The Best of Building Assets Together

Favorite Group Activities That Help Youth Succeed

Jolene L. Roehlkepartain

The Best of Building Assets Together:
Favorite Group Activities That Help Youth Succeed

The following are registered trademarks of Search Institute:
Search Institute® and Developmental Assets®.

Jolene L. Roehlkepartain
Search Institute Press, Minneapolis, MN
Copyright © 2008 by Search Institute

Printed on acid-free paper in the United States of America.

Search Institute

Minneapolis, MN 55413
www.searchinstitute.org
612-376-8955 • 877-240-7251

ISBN-13: 978-1-57482-159-8
ISBN-10: 1-57482-159-8

Credits
Editor: Alison Dotson
Book Design: Mighty Media
Production Coordinator: Mary Ellen Buscher

Library of Congress Cataloging-in-Publication Data
Roehlkepartain, Jolene L., 1962-
  The best of building assets together : favorite group activities
that help youth succeed / by Jolene L. Roehlkepartain.
      p. cm.
  Includes indexes.
  ISBN-13: 978-1-57482-159-8 (pbk. : alk. paper)
  ISBN-10: 1-57482-159-8 (pbk. : alk. paper)
  1. Youth--Conduct of life. 2. Youth--Life skills guides. 3. Values
in adolescence. I. Search Institute (Minneapolis, Minn.) II.
Title.
  BJ1661.R59 2008
  305.235--dc22
                  2007034210

About Search Institute Press
Search Institute Press is a division of Search Institute, a
nonprofit organization that offers leadership, knowledge,
and resources to promote positive youth development. Our
mission at Search Institute Press is to provide practical and
hope-filled resources to help create a world in which all young
people thrive. Our products are embedded in research, and
the 40 Developmental Assets®—qualities, experiences, and
relationships youth need to succeed—are a central focus of our
resources. Our logo, the SIP flower, is a symbol of the thriving
and healthy growth young people experience when they have
an abundance of assets in their lives.

Licensing and Copyright
The educational activity sheets in *The Best of Building Assets
Together: Favorite Group Activities That Help Youth Succeed*
may be copied as needed. For each copy, please respect the
following guidelines:

- Do not remove, alter, or obscure the Search Institute credit
  and copyright information on any activity sheet.

- Clearly differentiate any material you add for local
  distribution from material prepared by Search Institute.

- Do not alter the Search Institute material in content or
  meaning.

- Do not resell the activity sheets for profit.

- Include the following attribution when you use the
  information from the activity sheets in other formats for
  promotional or educational purposes: **Reprinted with
  permission from *The Best of Building Assets: Favorite
  Group Activities That Help Youth Succeed* (specify the
  title of the activity sheet you are quoting). Copyright
  © 2008 by Search Institute Press, Minneapolis,
  Minnesota, 877-240-7251, www.search-institute.org.
  All rights reserved.**

Printing Tips
Always copy from the original or print from the CD. Copying
from a copy lowers the reproduction quality. If you are using
more than one activity sheet or an activity sheet that runs
more than one page, make two-sided copies.

To Peter L. Benson (1949-2011), former president of Search Institute, who created the Developmental Assets® framework. Peter also wrote the Foreword for the first edition of *Building Assets Together* in 1995, saying "Developmental Assets are at the heart of the vision of helping young people grow up healthy, caring, and principled."

Table of Contents

Acknowledgments

Even though a book often lists one author, publishing a book requires the dedication and enthusiasm of many, many people. I would especially like to thank Tenessa Gemelke, Publishing Manager, who always has thoughtful guidance that makes each draft of the manuscript better. I also appreciate the fine work of Mary Ellen Buscher, Production Coordinator; Betsy Gabler, Publishing Sales Manager; Bill Kauffmann, Trade Sales Coordinator; and Alison Dotson, Assistant Editor. I also am indebted to the high-quality work of Rebecca Grothe, who wrote *More Building Assets Together*. A number of the best activities from that book are included in this one.

In addition, a number of asset-building individuals contributed to this book, either by reviewing it, offering suggestions, or sharing activities. These include: Jessica Andrews, who is part of GUIDE Inc. and the Georgia Teen Institutes in Lawrenceville, Georgia; Pamela J. Brock, who is in 4-H Youth Development in Elkhart, Indiana; Tammy Brothers, the director of Teen Student Leadership Academy, West Central Indiana ESC, Greencastle, Indiana; Rhiannon Carey, who works in the Human Development Center in Cloquet, Minnesota; Andrew Coonradt, a secondary social studies teacher, Newark, New York; Wendy Crocetti, the director of school-age programs, Hunterdon County YMCA, Alpha, New Jersey; Marsha Finkelstein, the coordinator of Teen Outreach Program (TOP), Health Quarters, Beverly, Massachusetts; Ray Fox, the chair of the Quakertown Healthy Community • Healthy Youth Organization in Quakertown, Pennsylvania; Pat Howell-Blackmore, who is part of Thrive! in Waterloo, Ontario; Angela Jerabek, the founder of the asset-building Ninth-Grade Program at St. Louis Park High School in St. Louis Park, Minnesota; Tricia Mayers, the head teacher of Trenton After School Program, Trenton, New Jersey; Buffy McNeal, the Developmental Assets District Team Chair in the Caribou schools in Caribou, Maine; Barbara A. Moore, former youth coordinator, St. Christopher Parish, Moreno Valley, California; Marilyn Peplau, a Wisconsin-based trainer through Vision Training Associates; Phyllis Phillips, youth minister, Blessed Kateri Youth Ministry, Sparta, New Jersey; James Robinson, the former director of Ohio County Together We Care, in Bowling Green, Kentucky; Flora Sanchez, a New Mexico–based Search Institute trainer through Vision Training Associates; Nancy Tellett-Royce, community liaison at Search Institute and member of Children First, the Executive Committee of the Healthy Communities • Healthy Youth initiative in St. Louis Park, Minnesota; Loran J. Thompson, a youth development consultant in San Diego; Robert Valois, professor, Health Promotion, Education & Behavior, Arnold School of Public Health, University of South Carolina, Columbia, South Carolina; James Vollbracht, an Arizona-based Search Institute trainer through Vision Training Associates; Liza Weidle, the former co-coordinator of Creating Assets Reaching Youth (CARY) in Cary, North Carolina; Janece Wooley-Woulard, who works with at-risk youth in Toledo, Ohio; and Susan Wootten, associate editor with Search Institute.

Whenever I'm with a group of young people during trainings or through my volunteer work, I marvel at the insights they have. My favorite activity in this book, the Web of Support (page 22), always brings out some new insight in young people.

When I recently used this activity with a group of teenagers, we were talking about what happens when countries work together instead of fighting each other. Each young person picked a different country to focus on, and after we had formed a web with the yarn, we began discussing what happens when one country pulls the strings too hard (and cuts off the "circulation" to another country), and what happens when one country refuses to cooperate and lets go.

Two young people in the group began arguing. When I asked them to quiet down, they said they couldn't—their countries had been invaded, and they weren't happy that a war was now being waged in their countries.

I asked what we should do, and one person mentioned this was why the United Nations had been founded. A discussion ensued about what was both effective and ineffective in the way the United Nations did its work.

I was proud that these young people were so aware of global affairs, but I kept trying to stretch them. "So what can *we* do?" Another discussion erupted and soon it became heated, but most of the talk was about how other people were making terrible choices.

"I mean *us*," I said again. "What can *we* do that will make a difference?"

That led our discussion to asset building and community building, which is where I believe most productive conversations are grounded. Too often, we feel so hopeless about what's happening *out there* that we don't do anything *here*.

I asked what the group could do to make a difference. I encouraged them to think metaphorically.

Which people in our organization or community are ignored or left out? We discussed a lot of ideas. The group finally narrowed their focus to the many elderly people in our community who reside in assisted living centers. One young person had a grandmother in one, and it bothered her how few people visited her grandmother and how most residents were ignored on holidays.

Valentine's Day was approaching, so the group decided to make simple Valentine baskets with candy and homemade cards to hang on the doorknobs of a nearby assisted living facility. We got permission from the facility and asked what guidelines we needed to follow.

The young people in the group were buoyant when delivering these baskets. Some giggled as they slid them onto doorknobs without being seen. Others went and hung out with some residents in the activity area. A week later, we were very surprised when we received a large thank-you note from the center. The baskets were a huge hit! Everybody at the center was talking about it, and they wanted to meet these marvelous young people.

Some of the young people became regulars at the center. One played the piano and led the residents in singing, and others played board games and Bingo with the residents. Relationships formed, and soon it became a place where the web of support was working, not only for the elderly but for the young people as well.

To me, that's what building Developmental Assets is all about: Bringing out the best in young people. Bringing out the best in our community. Bringing out the best in our world.

What Are Developmental Assets?

Search Institute has identified 40 positive experiences and qualities—Developmental Assets—that all of us have the power to bring into the lives of children and youth. The assets represent commonsense priorities for helping youth grow up healthy and successful. Twenty of the assets are external: interlocking systems of support, empowerment, boundaries and expectations, and constructive use of time. The remaining 20 assets are internal: the commitments, values, skills, and identity that guide young people in their choices.

The assets are spread across eight broad areas of human development. These categories paint a picture of the positive things that young people need to grow up healthy and responsible. A complete list of the Developmental Assets is provided on page 12.

The first four asset categories focus on external structures, relationships, and activities that create a positive environment for young people:

Support—Young people need to be surrounded by people who love, care for, appreciate, and accept

The Power of Assets

The 40 Developmental Assets represent common wisdom about the qualities of life that young people need and deserve, but the value of these assets extends further. Schools and communities that have surveyed their youth using Search Institute's *Profiles of Student Life: Attitudes & Behaviors* survey will find these activities particularly useful as they begin to explore and implement asset-promoting strategies. Surveys of more than 2.2 million young people in grades 6 through 12 reveal that assets are powerful influences on young people's behavior. Regardless of gender, ethnic heritage, economic situation, or geographic location, the assets not only promote positive behaviors and attitudes but also help protect young people from many different problem behaviors. The more assets young people have, the more likely they are to act in ways we value, such as succeeding in school and valuing diversity. The more assets young people have, the less likely they are to get into trouble or use alcohol and other drugs.

them. They need to know that they belong and that they are not alone.

Empowerment—Young people need to feel valued and valuable. This happens when youth feel safe, when they believe that they are liked and respected, and when they contribute to their families and communities.

Boundaries and Expectations—Young people need the positive influence of peers and adults who encourage them to be and do their best. Youth also need clear rules about appropriate behavior, and consistent, reasonable consequences for breaking those rules.

Constructive Use of Time—Young people need opportunities outside of school to learn and develop new skills and interests, and to spend enjoyable time interacting with other youth and adults.

The next four categories reflect internal values, skills, and beliefs that young people also need to develop in order to fully engage with and function in the world around them:

Commitment to Learning—Young people need a variety of learning experiences, including the desire for academic success, a sense of the lasting importance of learning, and a belief in their own abilities.

Positive Values—Young people need to develop strong guiding values or principles, including caring about others, having high standards for personal character, and believing in protecting their own well-being.

Social Competencies—Young people need to develop the skills to interact effectively with others, to make difficult decisions and choices, and to cope with new situations.

Positive Identity—Young people need to believe in their own self-worth, to feel that they have control over the things that happen to them, and to have a sense of purpose in life as well as a positive view of the future.

Many of these Developmental Assets are things that people already talk about and do on a daily basis. What's unique about them, though, is that the framework of assets draws together many different pieces so that they are understandable and make sense together.

Furthermore, research underscores the incredible power of these assets in young people's lives. When young people have more of these Developmental Assets, they are much more likely to lead healthy, positive, productive lives. They simply do not make as many harmful decisions as youth who don't have these assets. They have fewer problems with alcohol and other drugs, violence, and sexual involvement.

When youth have more Developmental Assets, they are more likely to engage in positive behaviors and less likely to engage in unhealthy behaviors. In short, an increase in assets means a decrease in the crises young people may face, so the crises don't consume everyone's energy. Thus, by promoting assets, we spend less time dealing with the fallout from problems that may otherwise result and more time enjoying youth's gifts.

How to Use This Book

The Best of Building Assets Together is a collection of group activities and reproducible handouts that help young people explore their lives and set goals to make their dreams come true. Through active and interactive learning, reflection, projects, and worksheets, young people learn about the importance of assets, strengths in their lives, sources of support, and areas for growth. These activities and handouts help young people understand the important things they need to grow up healthy, empowering them to take charge and make wise choices for themselves and have a positive impact on the lives of others.

Who Should Read This Book

People in many settings have found the assets valuable in understanding and working with youth. Because we hope to reach a broad audience, we have used language that we feel will be understood most widely. As you read through the book, you may need or want to customize activities to fit your specific setting or goals. The activities have been developed to be useful to people who are involved with youth in schools (classrooms, advisory groups), community organizations (recreation programs, clubs, sports teams), and congregations (youth groups, religious education, retreats). The activities are designed to be used with youth in grades 6 through 12. Depending on the maturity and interests of the youth you work with, you may find that some activities are more appropriate for younger youth, while others may be more applicable to older youth. Adapt the activities to best meet the needs of your group of young people. Older youth might even serve as role models and tutors for younger youth with the structure provided within the activities.

The Best of Building Assets Together includes the best activities and handouts from two previous best-selling books: *Building Assets Together* and *More Building Assets Together*. Experts and practitioners who work with young people gave extensive feedback on which activities were most effective and how to strengthen them. Some even shared additional ideas that appear in the "My Idea" sidebars throughout the book. You'll also find more than 35 new activities and handouts that offer fresh ideas for group activities.

Ways to Use This Book

Most of these activities can be completed in less than 30 minutes. Use them in whatever way will best fit your needs. Here are some possibilities:

- **Pick and choose individual activities** as they fit into the ongoing plans for your group. Integrate them into existing objectives, plans, and/or curriculum.

- **Combine several activities** for an entire session, meeting, or retreat devoted to learning about a specific topic.

40 Developmental Assets

Search Institute has identified the following building blocks of healthy development that help young people grow up healthy, caring, and responsible.

ASSET TYPE | **ASSET NAME AND DEFINITION**

EXTERNAL

Support

1. **Family Support**—Family life provides high levels of love and support.
2. **Positive Family Communication**—Young person and her or his parent(s) communicate positively, and young person is willing to seek advice and counsel from parents.
3. **Other Adult Relationships**—Young person receives support from three or more nonparent adults.
4. **Caring Neighborhood**—Young person experiences caring neighbors.
5. **Caring School Climate**—School provides a caring, encouraging environment.
6. **Parent Involvement in Schooling**—Parent(s) are actively involved in helping young person succeed in school.

Empowerment

7. **Community Values Youth**—Young person perceives that adults in the community value youth.
8. **Youth as Resources**—Young people are given useful roles in the community.
9. **Service to Others**—Young person serves in the community one hour or more per week.
10. **Safety**—Young person feels safe at home, school, and in the neighborhood.

Boundaries and Expectations

11. **Family Boundaries**—Family has clear rules and consequences and monitors the young person's whereabouts.
12. **School Boundaries**—School provides clear rules and consequences.
13. **Neighborhood Boundaries**—Neighbors take responsibility for monitoring young people's behavior.
14. **Adult Role Models**—Parent(s) and other adults model positive, responsible behavior.
15. **Positive Peer Influence**—Young person's best friends model responsible behavior.
16. **High Expectations**—Both parent(s) and teachers encourage the young person to do well.

Constructive Use of Time

17. **Creative Activities**—Young person spends three or more hours per week in lessons or practice in music, theater, or other arts.
18. **Youth Programs**—Young person spends three or more hours per week in sports, clubs, or organizations at school and/or in the community.
19. **Religious Community**—Young person spends one or more hours per week in activities in a religious institution.
20. **Time at Home**—Young person is out with friends "with nothing special to do" two or fewer nights per week.

INTERNAL

Commitment to Learning

21. **Achievement Motivation**—Young person is motivated to do well in school.
22. **School Engagement**—Young person is actively engaged in learning.
23. **Homework**—Young person reports doing at least one hour of homework every school day.
24. **Bonding to School**—Young person cares about her or his school.
25. **Reading for Pleasure**—Young person reads for pleasure three or more hours per week.

Positive Values

26. **Caring**—Young person places high value on helping other people.
27. **Equality and Social Justice**—Young person places high value on promoting equality and reducing hunger and poverty.
28. **Integrity**—Young person acts on convictions and stands up for her or his beliefs.
29. **Honesty**—Young person "tells the truth even when it is not easy."
30. **Responsibility**—Young person accepts and takes personal responsibility.
31. **Restraint**—Young person believes it is important not to be sexually active or to use alcohol or other drugs.

Social Competencies

32. **Planning and Decision Making**—Young person knows how to plan ahead and make choices.
33. **Interpersonal Competence**—Young person has empathy, sensitivity, and friendship skills.
34. **Cultural Competence**—Young person has knowledge of and comfort with people of different cultural/racial/ethnic backgrounds.
35. **Resistance Skills**—Young person can resist negative peer pressure and dangerous situations.
36. **Peaceful Conflict Resolution**—Young person seeks to resolve conflict nonviolently.

Positive Identity

37. **Personal Power**—Young person feels he or she has control over "things that happen to me."
38. **Self-Esteem**—Young person reports having a high self-esteem.
39. **Sense of Purpose**—Young person reports that "my life has a purpose."
40. **Positive View of Personal Future**—Young person is optimistic about her or his personal future.

- **Use activities in intergenerational settings** to help youth and adults explore together the importance of Developmental Assets.
- **Encourage youth participants** to select activities to use with peers or younger children.
- **Create a notebook** about the Developmental Assets for each young person, photocopying the worksheets provided throughout the book.
- **Keep the discussion going** to help young people process what they've experienced and learned. The discussion questions throughout this book are based on the service-learning discussion model of reflecting on *what* (what happened), *so what* (why this is important), and *now what* (which steps we take next).

There are no instant or magical ways to build Developmental Assets. They are nurtured in numerous ways through a young person's positive relationships with many people. The activities in this resource provide opportunities for engaging in meaningful conversations that can strengthen relationships. Young people will be encouraged not only to learn about the assets but also to understand how they can build them for themselves and with other youth. The real power comes when young people apply what they learn from their group experiences to their own lives.

How This Book Is Organized

The Best of Building Assets Together is organized into chapters around major emphases that schools and organizations value and teach. The first chapter includes activities that introduce youth to the concept of Developmental Assets and invites them to consider the Developmental Assets framework as a whole. The first activity begins with a self-analysis that introduces all 40 assets. Youth can see how other young people—148,189 of them, to be exact—responded to similar survey questions about their own assets.

Each remaining chapter presents many activities and handouts for these major topics:

- Icebreakers (or getting-to-know-you activities)
- Raising self-awareness

- Building skills
- Promoting leadership
- Strengthening relationships
- Improving communication
- Developing character
- Promoting diversity
- Setting goals, hopes, and dreams
- Becoming involved in the community

All the activities and handouts in this book build multiple assets. If you're interested in being intentional about building specific assets, use the Developmental Asset Index starting on page 152 to find activities and handouts that build those specific assets. English and Spanish versions of all the handouts in this book are available as downloads at Search Institute's website. To access them, go to **www.search-institute.org/oc/bestofbat**.

Leading Groups of Young People

All the activities in this book are designed to be positive experiences for youth. However, discussions of assets may evoke strong feelings and reactions, both positive and negative. Some activities can lead to difficult discussions, especially when they're used with youth who have few assets or with particularly vulnerable youth, such as young people from difficult homes and those acting out in troubling ways, such as skipping school or smoking. Be sensitive to young people's concerns, and adapt the activities and reflection questions to fit your situation and your educational goals. Don't force youth to participate in any of these activities. Invite all youth to share their ideas and feedback about the assets and the activities.

Here are some things to keep in mind as you prepare for an activity, facilitate the discussion, and interact with young people:

- Identify the purposes for each gathering. Is the group building community, learning, planning, or completing a project? Help the group stay on task, but be careful not to be so task-oriented that young people do not have enough time and space for discussion and exploration.

Paying Attention to Group Dynamics

Carefully observe the interpersonal dynamics in your group each time you meet. As you observe the group in action, ask yourself questions such as:

- Who tries to keep the group interactions on a friendly note?
- Who seems to thrive on conflict and disagreement?
- Who seems involved and interested?
- Do any youth seem uninvolved or disconnected from the group? If so, how can you help them connect?
- Are there any subgroups? Which youth routinely agree and support each other or consistently disagree and oppose each other?
- What brings out the best in your group of young people?

Building Developmental Assets is an important strategy for schools, youth-serving organizations, congregations, families, and communities. By using these activities with youth, you can help young people focus their thinking and priorities. In doing so, you can contribute in a significant way to helping them succeed—both now and in the future.

- Learn the name of each young person and say it aloud at least twice during your time together. Ideally greet and say good-bye to each individual in the group by name. Challenge group members to know each other, and you, by name as well.
- As a group, decide on appropriate ground rules for behavior.
- Reaffirm the goals and mission of your group each time you meet.
- Provide warmth, acceptance, and concern for each individual in your group.
- Find ways to support each individual as well as the entire group on a regular basis.

- Provide feedback to individuals or the entire group in ways that are respectful and helpful.
- Help young people translate their feelings and experiences into ideas.
- Learn with your young people. You do not have to be an expert or know all the answers. Do not be too quick to share what you know. Let the group discover new learning together. When you do contribute knowledge or information that you have, do so in ways that will enhance the group discussion, not shut it down.
- Be honest as you share about yourself and your feelings. Model acceptance, openness, and trust as you encourage youth to share their feelings and experiences with each other.
- Be a model of good active listening skills.
- Let the group wrestle with tough situations and discover how their own resources can pull them through a rough spot. Intervene sparingly.
- Be aware of different comfort levels among youth. Some young people are very shy or may have discomfort with physical contact. Adjust activities as needed to respect personal boundaries.
- At the end of each gathering, help the group summarize and consider new learning to take with them. Identify follow-up action that would be helpful.

My Idea: *"We created the St. Louis Park Building Assets–Reducing Risks Program to help students make a successful transition to high school. Students really enjoy the asset-building activities, and they become engaged in the school, with their teachers, and with their peers in a unique way."*

—Angie Jerabek, St. Louis Park, Minnesota

1
Building Developmental Assets

To grow up well and succeed in life, young people need Developmental Assets. Minneapolis-based Search Institute has identified 40 Developmental Assets that all young people need to become caring, principled individuals who bring out the best in others while bringing out the best in themselves. This chapter presents activities and ready-to-use handouts that will help young people understand the Developmental Assets framework and the ways they can build assets in themselves and in others.

Focus: Youth analyze their own assets and compare their responses to those of 148,189 other youth who have been surveyed by Search Institute.

Developmental Assets Tie-in:

The Developmental Assets Framework

You will need:

• copies of "An Asset Checklist" from page 17, "Developmental Assets among Youth" from page 18, and "The Power of Developmental Assets" from page 19—one for each youth

Activity: Distribute the worksheet "An Asset Checklist" (p. 17) for each youth to fill out. Assure them that no one will look at their responses, so they can be completely honest. Tell them they should share only what they feel comfortable sharing. After youth finish, have them compare their responses to the "Developmental Assets among Youth" (page 18).

Discussion Questions:

• *Most young people experience many of these assets. The top five assets that most youth report having in their lives are: 21–Achievement Motivation (75%), 28–Integrity (75%), 1–Family Support (73%), 40–Positive View of Personal Future (73%), 15–Positive Peer Influence (72%).*

How do your assets compare with those of other young people? In what ways are your assets similar to and different from youth surveyed? Why do you think that is?

• *Most young people are also missing certain other assets. The five assets that most youth do not have in their lives are: 17– Creative Activities (20%), 25–Reading for Pleasure (22%), 7–Community Values Youth (25%), 8–Youth as Resources (32%), and 14–Adult Role Models (32%), and 14–Adult Role Models (32%).*

How many of these assets do you have in your life? How important do you think these assets are? Why? Why do you think researchers have said they are important in growing up healthy?

• *The assets are separated into internal assets and external assets. Assets 1–20 are external assets. They're the assets that are built by your relationships with friends, family members, community members, and organizations: Support, Empowerment, Boundaries and Expectations, and Constructive Use of Time. Assets 21–40 are internal assets. These are the assets that help you make wise choices: Commitment to Learning, Positive Values, Social Competencies, and Positive Identity. Do you have more internal assets or external assets? Why do you think that is?*

• *Research shows that the average teenager has only about 20 of these assets. Look at how many assets for which you checked "true." How do you compare to other youth? Are you more similar or more different? Also compare your number of assets to other students' in your grade (see box). Why do you think older youth have fewer assets than younger youth?*

• *Research reveals that the more assets you have, the more likely you are to succeed. (Distribute the handout "The Power of Developmental Assets" [p. 19].) What happens to risky behaviors, such as alcohol use and sexual activity, when the number of assets a young person has goes up? What happens to positive behaviors, such as school success and exhibiting leadership, when the number of assets a young person has goes up? What does this handout make you think about the power of these Developmental Assets?*

Assets by Grade

In the study of over 120,000 youth, the number of assets youth experience by grade are as follows:

All	20.6
Grade 6	23.7
Grade 7	22.7
Grade 8	21.3
Grade 9	20.5
Grade 10	19.6
Grade 11	19.5
Grade 12	19.4

Many young people experience too few of the Developmental Assets.
Read each statement below and check whether it is true or false in your own life.

External Assets

Support
True False

1. I receive lots of love and support from my family. ☐ ☐
2. My parent(s) and I communicate positively, and I am willing to go to my parent(s) for advice and counsel. ☐ ☐
3. I receive support from three or more nonparent adults. ☐ ☐
4. I have caring neighbors. ☐ ☐
5. My school provides a caring, encouraging environment. ☐ ☐
6. My parent(s) are actively involved in helping me succeed in school. ☐ ☐

Empowerment

7. I believe that adults in my community value youth. ☐ ☐
8. I believe that young people are given useful roles in my community. ☐ ☐
9. I serve in my community for one hour or more per week. ☐ ☐
10. I feel safe at home, at school, and in the neighborhood. ☐ ☐

Boundaries and Expectations

11. My family has clear rules and consequences, and monitors my whereabouts. ☐ ☐
12. My school provides clear rules and consequences. ☐ ☐
13. My neighbors take responsibility for monitoring young people's behavior. ☐ ☐
14. Parent(s) and other adults model positive, responsible behavior. ☐ ☐
15. My best friends model responsible behavior. ☐ ☐
16. Both my parent(s) and my teachers encourage me to do well. ☐ ☐

Constructive Use of Time

17. I spend three hours or more per week in lessons or practice in music, theater, or other arts. ☐ ☐
18. I spend three hours or more per week in sports, clubs, organizations at school, and/or in community organizations. ☐ ☐
19. I spend one or more hours per week in activities in a religious institution. ☐ ☐
20. I go out with friends "with nothing special to do" no more than two nights per week. ☐ ☐

Internal Assets

Commitment to Learning
True False

21. I am motivated to do well in school. ☐ ☐
22. I am actively engaged in learning. ☐ ☐
23. I do at least one hour of homework every school day. ☐ ☐
24. I care about my school. ☐ ☐
25. I read for pleasure three or more hours per week. ☐ ☐

Positive Values

26. I place a high value on helping other people. ☐ ☐
27. I place a high value on promoting equality and reducing hunger and poverty. ☐ ☐
28. I act on my convictions and stand up for my beliefs. ☐ ☐
29. I tell the truth even when it is not easy. ☐ ☐
30. I accept responsibilities and take personal responsibility for my actions. ☐ ☐
31. I believe it is important not to be sexually active or to use alcohol or other drugs. ☐ ☐

Social Competencies

32. I know how to plan ahead and make choices. ☐ ☐
33. I have empathy, sensitivity, and friendship skills. ☐ ☐
34. I have knowledge of and comfort with people of different cultural/racial/ethnic backgrounds. ☐ ☐
35. I can resist negative peer pressure and dangerous situations. ☐ ☐
36. I seek to resolve conflict nonviolently. ☐ ☐

Positive Identity

37. I feel I have control over things that happen to me. ☐ ☐
38. I have a high self-esteem. ☐ ☐
39. I believe my life has a purpose. ☐ ☐
40. I am optimistic about my personal future. ☐ ☐

Developmental Assets Tie-in:
The Developmental Assets Framework

Search Institute surveyed more than 120,000 youth in grades 6 through 12. The percentages of youth who report having each asset are as follows:

Developmental Assets Tie-in:

The Developmental Assets Framework

1. Family Support 73%		**21.** Achievement Motivation 75%
2. Positive Family Communication 33%		**22.** School Engagement 63%
3. Other Adult Relationships 52%		**23.** Homework 54%
4. Caring Neighborhood 38%		**24.** Bonding to School 64%
5. Caring School Climate 37%		**25.** Reading for Pleasure 22%
6. Parent Involvement in Schooling 32%		**26.** Caring 58%
7. Community Values Youth 25%		**27.** Equality and Social Justice 60%
8. Youth as Resources 32%		**28.** Integrity 75%
9. Service to Others 52%		**29.** Honesty 71%
10. Safety 53%		**30.** Responsibility 70%
11. Family Boundaries 46%		**31.** Restraint 47%
12. School Boundaries 57%		**32.** Planning and Decision Making 36%
13. Neighborhood Boundaries 46%		**33.** Interpersonal Competence 48%
14. Adult Role Models 32%		**34.** Cultural Competence 45%
15. Positive Peer Influence 72%		**35.** Resistance Skills 48%
16. High Expectations 57%		**36.** Peaceful Conflict Resolution 49%
17. Creative Activities 20%		**37.** Personal Power 44%
18. Youth Programs 65%		**38.** Self-Esteem 49%
19. Religious Community 49%		**39.** Sense of Purpose 61%
20. Time at Home 64%		**40.** Positive View of Personal Future 73%

**Developmental
Assets Tie-in:**

The Developmental
Assets Framework

HIGH-RISK BEHAVIOR PATTERNS

PERCENT AT RISK

Category	Definition	Total	If 0–10 Assets	If 11–20 Assets	If 21–30 Assets	If 31–40 Assets
Problem Alcohol Use	Has used alcohol three or more times in the last 30 days or got drunk once or more in the last two weeks	17%	39%	22%	10%	2%
Marijuana Use	Used marijuana or hashish once or more times in the past 30 days.	13%	35%	17%	6%	1%
Sexual Activity	Has had sexual intercourse three or more times in lifetime	15%	31%	20%	10%	3%
Violence	Has engaged in three or more acts of fighting, hitting, injuring a person, carrying a weapon, or threatening physical harm in the past 12 months.	22%	53%	27%	11%	3%
School Problems	Has skipped school two or more days in the last four weeks and/or has below a C average	15%	38%	18%	8%	3%

POSITIVE BEHAVIORS

PERCENT INVOLVED

Category	Definition	Total	If 0–10 Assets	If 11–20 Assets	If 21–30 Assets	If 31–40 Assets
Suceeds in School	Gets mostly As on report card	31%	10%	23%	39%	57%
Values Diversity	Thinks it is important to get to know people of other racial/ethnic groups	60%	32%	53%	69%	84%
Maintains Good Health	Takes good care of body (such as eating foods that are healthy, and exercises regularly)	61%	29%	50%	73%	91%
Exhibits Leadership	Has been a leader of a group or organization in the last 12 months	72%	50%	68%	79%	86%

Based on a sample of more than 120,000 youth in grades 6 through 12. Copyright © 2017 by Search Institute ®.

5 | Announcing, Announcing

Focus: Youth create announcements that encourage other youth to build assets.

Developmental Assets Tie-in:

The Developmental Assets Framework

You will need:

• pencils or pens

• writing paper

• large clock with a second hand (or watches with second hands)

• copies of the list of the 40 Developmental Assets from page 12

• masking tape

Activity: Write each of the eight asset categories in large print on eight sheets of writing paper. Post the sheets around the room.

Create pairs by asking youth to find another person who is wearing the same color that they are wearing. Station each pair at one of the eight sheets. (Try to have all the categories covered.) Give each pair a copy of the 40 Developmental Assets. Have pairs of youth write 30-second announcements that will inspire their peers to build assets. For example, a group might create an announcement based on a single asset, such as how doing your homework every day will help you succeed. Or a group might use the entire asset framework: "If you want support, give support. If you want to be empowered, empower a friend."

Allow time for each pair to share their announcement with the group.

Discussion Questions:

• *What are the most effective ways to motivate your peers to do something that you think is important?*

• *How do we know which messages motivate students?*

• *Why is it important for people to build assets?*

• *What do people need to know about the Developmental Assets before they are likely to support the idea of asset building?*

My Idea: *"Have people pair up and talk about an asset they're really good at building. I call it Brag a Bit. Have them talk about how they build this asset and to give an example. The other person practices listening and asking questions."*
—James Vollbracht, Tucson, Arizona

---

6 | Alphabet Review

Focus: Teams compete to compose a list of ideas for building assets.

Developmental Assets Tie-in:

The Developmental Assets Framework

You will need:

• eight pieces of newsprint

• masking tape

• a noisemaker

• pencils or pens

Activity: Turn newsprint sideways so it's wider than it is high. Label each newsprint with three letters of the alphabet, starting with A, B, and C and omitting X and Z. Leave room for youth to write under each letter. Hang the eight pieces of newsprint around the room with masking tape.

Create four teams of youth according to birth month (January–March, April–June, July–September, October–December). Station each team near different pieces of newsprint—ideally the groups will be spaced evenly throughout the room. Give each person a pencil or pen.

Ask the young people to think of asset-building actions that begin with the letters on their newsprint (such as: **A**sk others for help when you need it, **B**e a good listener, **C**are), and write one idea under each letter. In the next minute, ask youth to write as many actions under each alphabet letter as they can.

After one minute, sound the noisemaker and tell teams to move to the newsprint on their right. Repeat this each minute until every team has written on all eight pieces of newsprint.

Discussion Questions:

• *What new or unexpected ideas did you discover?*

• *How could we share these good ideas with others? (Plan to take action on these as appropriate for your setting.)*

• *Which idea would you try in your own life?*

7 | The Supports Around You

Developmental Assets Tie-in:

1—Family Support
3—Other Adult Relationships
4—Caring Neighborhood
14—Adult Role Models
15—Positive Peer Influence

Think about the people in your life. Who supports you? Think about your parent(s), extended family members, teachers, neighbors, friends, coaches, employers—anyone you think is supportive. Write your name in the middle circle below. Then write the names of supportive people that you know and trust in the surrounding circles, with one name in each circle. If you want to include more than eight people, draw more circles and add those names. After you finish, circle the person you feel closest to.

Then choose one of the people you would like to get to know better and decorate that circle so that it stands out from the others. In the next two weeks, do one thing to let that person know that he or she is important to you. You can call the person on the phone, visit the person, or send a letter or e-mail.

Consider choosing a different person to reach out to each month.

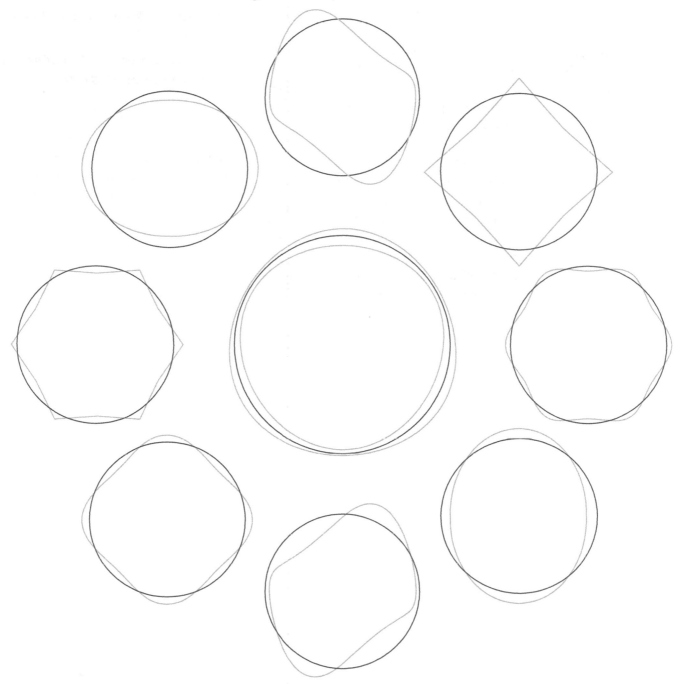

8 | Web of Support

Focus: Youth identify various sources of support in their lives.

Developmental Assets Tie-in:

1—Family Support
3—Other Adult Relationships
4—Caring Neighborhood
5—Caring School Climate

You will need:

• a beach ball or other type of "blow-up" ball

• enough yarn to make a web

Activity: Have youth sit in a circle; then give one youth a ball of yarn. Ask that young person to name one person who supports her or him and how. Then ask the youth to hold the end of the string and throw the rest of the ball to another person in the circle. The youth who catches the ball of yarn should then name a person who supports her or him and how before holding an end of the yarn and throwing the ball to someone else. As the activity continues, a web that connects all the youth will appear. Make sure that all of the young people get to participate at least once.

After a web has been spun and youth begin to run out of people to name, explain to them that the beach ball represents young people and the web of yarn represents the support system made up of all the people they mentioned. Toss the beach ball into the web and encourage the youth to move it around without letting it slip through the gaps in the web. If the web cannot support the beach ball, continue listing additional supportive people and adding to the web (with each participant holding two strands) until the beach ball bounces easily without falling through.

Discussion Questions:

• How many different types of people did we name (family, friends, neighbors)?

• Is it more important to you to have lots of different people who are somewhat supportive or just a few who are very supportive? Why?

• What happens when the gaps in our webs of support are too wide?

• What attributes do supportive people have that are important to you?

• If someone you know seemed to need more support, how would you suggest that he or she find it?

My Idea: *"This activity gives such a good visual. At the end, I always have a person drop out of supporting the web, which gives that final vision of why it is so important to stay involved with youth."*
—Liza Weidle, Cary, North Carolina

Who builds your assets? Where are they built? Circle the people and places where you believe your Developmental Assets are being nurtured and strengthened.

Developmental Assets Tie-in:

The Developmental Assets Framework

ASSET-BUILDING PEOPLE

Mom	Grandmother	Uncle
Neighbor	Janitor	**Youth director**
Dad	Grandfather	**Club leader**
Teacher	Counselor	Librarian
Sister	Aunt	Music teacher
COACH	Clergy	Friend
Brother	Art teacher	**Mentor**
Bus driver	My parent's friend	Principal

ASSET-BUILDING PLACES

SCHOOL	COFFEE OR ICE CREAM SHOP
Home	Park
After-school program	My community
My neighborhood	My parent's work
GYM	Bike or walking trail
My work	Restaurant
Music Hall	My friend's home
Congregation	Recreation center
LIBRARY	Theater

10 | Boundaries and Expectations

Focus: Youth evaluate which boundaries and expectations are important to them.

Developmental Assets Tie-in:

11—Family Boundaries
12—School Boundaries
13—Neighborhood Boundaries
16—High Expectations

You will need:

• dot labels (self-adhesive "sticky dots")

• markers

• newsprint

Activity: Label one piece of newsprint "Important Boundaries" and the other "Important Expectations." Post these in your meeting space, some distance from each other.

Draw the group's attention to the charts you've hung and explain what you mean by "boundaries" and "expectations." When everyone has a good grasp of the terminology, ask them to think quietly for a moment about the rules or boundaries that are most important to them, their families, and their school. Then ask them to think for a moment about the most important positive expectations they have for themselves and that their families and schools have for them. Allow a few minutes for youth to write two or three responses on each of the charts.

After everyone has written on the charts, give each youth five sticky dots to mark the items on the list that he or she thinks are most important. Tally and make a chart of the top three boundaries and the top three expectations.

Discussion Questions:

• *What did you discover about boundaries and expectations?*

• *How important is it that your family, school, and community have similar boundaries and expectations for you? Why?*

• *What boundaries and expectations do you set for yourself? Why?*

• *What can we do about the mixed messages youth receive about boundaries and expectations?*

11 | Time for What?

Focus: Youth talk about how they spend their time each day.

Developmental Assets Tie-in:

17—Creative Activities
18—Youth Programs
19—Religious Community
20—Time at Home
23—Homework

You will need:

• newsprint (at least 13 sheets)

• markers

• masking tape

Activity: Have teams of youth make a sign for each of the following categories (or others that are appropriate for your group): Sleep, Eat, School, Work, Homework, Extracurricular Activities, Religious Activities, Spend Time with Friends, Spend Time with Family, Spend Time Online, Play Video Games, Have Alone Time, and Watch Television. Have youth hang each of these signs on the walls of your room using masking tape. Spread the signs throughout the room.

Then say something like: "Now, everyone stand in the middle of the room. I'm going to start naming hours of the day. Think about what you're usually doing at that time, then run to the appropriate sign and stand there until I name another time of day—then you'll switch to something else. Ready? Let's begin.

"Pretend it's one minute past midnight on a Wednesday night during the school year. Where are you? [Pause.] How about 1 a.m.? [Pause.] 2 a.m.? [Pause.] 3 a.m.? [Pause.]"

Continue naming each hour until you get back to midnight. Watch where youth congregate and for how long. Then repeat the activity, using a weekend day.

Discussion Questions:

• *Where do you spend most of your time on school days? Why?*

• *Where do you spend most of your time on the weekends? Why?*

• *Are there other things you spend lots of time doing that aren't included in the signs in this room? What are they?*

• *What kinds of activities do you do that are challenging and stimulating?*

• *What do you consider to be a big waste of time? Why?*

• *If you could choose how much time you would spend on each activity, which activities would you shorten? Why? Which ones would you lengthen? Why?*

12 | Where Are the Asset Builders?

Think about an organization, club, or group in which you participate. What are some of the things you gain from being involved and interacting with adults and other youth? Which assets does the organization, club, or group help build? How?

Developmental Assets Tie-in:

5—Caring School Climate
17—Creative Activities
18—Youth Programs
19—Religious Community

An organization or group that is important to me

How individuals in this group build assets for and with me

Ways I can give back to the group through service or building assets for others

Specific assets that this group builds

13 | Committed to Learning

Focus: Youth create slogans to encourage educational commitment.

Developmental Assets Tie-in:

21—Achievement Motivation
22—School Engagement
23—Homework
24—Bonding to School
25—Reading for Pleasure

You will need:

• five sheets of poster board

• markers

• pencils

• masking tape

Activity: Form five teams. Give each team a piece of poster board, markers, pencils, and masking tape. Assign each team one of these assets:

• 21—I am motivated to do well in school.

• 22—I am actively engaged in learning.

• 23—I do at least one hour of homework every school day.

• 24—I care about my school.

• 25—I read for pleasure three or more hours per week.

Have each team create a catchy slogan to put on its poster board (think of it as a billboard) that reflects the asset the team has been given. For example, the team with asset 22 might write "Be All You Can Be: Keep Learning Every Day"; the team with asset 23 might write "Do your homework every day, and you'll succeed in every way"; and the team with asset 25 might write: "Read. Read. Read. And you'll go far, far, far." Encourage teams to be creative and spend time designing their posters. Have teams show their "billboards" to the whole group.

Discussion Questions:

• *Which of these slogans is easiest for you to follow? Which is hardest? Why?*

• *Who are the people in your life who encourage you to keep learning?*

• *When you feel like giving up, what can you do to build up your commitment to learning?*

After the discussion, hang the billboards in your classroom, meeting room, or the hallway.

14 | Custom License Plates

Focus: Youth create messages about values.

Developmental Assets Tie-in:

26—Caring
27—Equality and Social Justice
28—Integrity
29—Honesty
30—Responsibility
31—Restraint

You will need:

• easel

• list of the six Positive Values assets

• markers

• newsprint

• tape

• white construction paper cut to the size of car license plates (one per participant)

Activity: Ask youth if they have ever seen customized or "vanity" license plates and if they can recall any of them. Give some examples of personalized messages you have noticed to jog their memories.

Challenge pairs of youth to create messages that promote the importance of the six values named in the Positive Values assets (assets 26–31). Explain that real license plates can use a combination of only nine letters and numbers, so youth must find creative ways to share their messages. Share an example such as "LUV2SK8" instead of "Love to Skate."

Give the pairs some time to brainstorm before they write their messages on the paper license plates you have provided. Encourage each pair to design at least two license plates. When everyone has finished writing, have each pair show its license plates to the larger group. Have each pair ask the other youth if they can tell what the combinations of letters and numbers mean and if they can guess the related asset, and then have pairs explain their thinking behind the message they created.

Discussion Questions:

• *Of the license plates that were created, which are your favorites? Why?*

• *Why should we promote positive values?*

• *How else do people show what they value?*

• *How do you show your values?*

Bonus Idea: Display these creations with others on a "Road to Positive Values" bulletin board or hallway mural.

Developmental Assets Tie-in:

The Developmental Assets Framework

Below are 40 statements describing different ways people may experience assets. Talk with people to find out which of these assets they have. Have them sign their initials in the box below where that statement is true for them. Try to find as many different people to sign your sheet as possible. If your group is large enough, try to find 40 people who fit these 40 different statements.

1: I have a grandparent who adores me.	**9:** I have done a service project.	**17:** I participate in music, art, or theater.	**25:** I love to read.	**33:** I know how to make friends.
2: It's easy to talk with my parent(s).	**10:** I feel safe.	**18:** I belong to a club.	**26:** I help other people.	**34:** I feel comfortable around people of all ethnicities.
3: I know a great teacher.	**11:** My parent(s) set clear rules and consequences.	**19:** I attend a religious organization.	**27:** I care about reducing hunger and poverty.	**35:** I can say no to negative peer pressure.
4: I am friends with a neighbor.	**12:** My school sets clear rules and consequences.	**20:** I spend time at home with my family.	**28:** I stand up for my beliefs.	**36:** I try to resolve conflicts nonviolently.
5: My school is a caring place.	**13:** I know my neighborhood's rules and consequences.	**21:** I want to do well in school.	**29:** I tell the truth.	**37:** I feel I have control over things that happen to me.
6: My parent(s) are involved at my school.	**14:** I have an adult role model.	**22:** I enjoy learning.	**30:** I take responsibility.	**38:** I have a high self-esteem.
7: I feel valued by my community.	**15:** I have a friend who brings out the best in me.	**23:** I always get my homework done on time.	**31:** I do not use drugs or alcohol.	**39:** My life has a purpose.
8: I have useful roles in my community.	**16:** Adults encourage me to do my best.	**24:** I care about my school.	**32:** I plan ahead.	**40:** I am optimistic about my future.

16 | Worthwhile Role Models

Focus: Youth analyze the social competencies of positive role models.

Developmental Assets Tie-in:

14—Adult Role Models
32—Planning and Decision Making
33—Interpersonal Competence
34—Cultural Competence
35—Resistance Skills
36—Peaceful Conflict Resolution

You will need:

• four sheets of poster board

• markers

• pencils

• masking tape

Activity: Ask your group to name six real-life positive role models they look up to (make sure you have both females and males). Then have youth form six small teams. Ask each team to pick one of the six role models and discuss that person. Explain that social competencies are like strengths, then ask youth to analyze that role model's social competencies by looking at assets 32 through 36. If youth wish to do more study, they can research magazine and newspaper articles about their role models and find out more about their personal habits, values, and skills. Then have a follow-up session where youth role-play the role models (emphasizing their social competencies) on a mock talk show.

Discussion Questions:

• *Which strengths seem to be most common among these role models? Are there any strengths they need to develop more?*

• *In what ways do these strengths help our role models succeed?*

• *Which strengths do you think you already have? Which would you like to develop?*

• *If these role models were in the room with us, what do you think they would tell us about ways to build these strengths in ourselves?*

17 | Inflated or Deflated?

Focus: Balloons symbolize how youth feel that others affect their identity.

Developmental Assets Tie-in:

37—Personal Power
38—Self-Esteem
39—Sense of Purpose
40—Positive View of Personal Future

You will need:

• chalkboard and chalk (or newsprint and markers)

• enough balloons for every participant

Activity: Give each youth a balloon. Tell them to blow once into the balloon each time you mention something that helps them feel good about themselves and let out a little air each time you mention something that makes them doubt or feel bad about themselves.

Then say the following statements:
Someone . . .
• takes your needs seriously
• gives you a hug
• laughs at your jokes
• takes advantage of you
• discriminates against you
• trusts you with a secret
• believes you can do something and tells you so
• rejects you
• thanks you for doing something for her or him
• expects too much of you and you can't meet those expectations
• calls you names
• ignores you
• forgives you
• invites you to do something exciting

Discussion Questions:

• *How did you feel as you watched your balloon become bigger? Smaller?*

• *Did some people deflate their balloons quietly while others did so loudly? Why? How is that similar to how people act in real-life situations?*

• *What would your balloon look like right now if I asked you to inflate it to match your level of self-esteem? Would it be large or small? Why?*

• *How can we encourage each other to keep our balloons large and full?*

Developmental Assets Tie-in:

The Developmental Assets Framework

Review this list of the 40 Developmental Assets. Which ones are current strengths in your life? Mark your five strongest assets with a star. Draw a large star next to the one asset that you would consider to be your strongest asset.

1. **Family Support**—Family life provides high levels of love and support.
2. **Positive Family Communication**—Young person and her or his parent(s) communicate positively, and young person is willing to seek advice and counsel from parent(s).
3. **Other Adult Relationships**—Young person receives support from three or more nonparent adults.
4. **Caring Neighborhood**—Young person experiences caring neighbors
5. **Caring School Climate**—School provides a caring, encouraging environment.
6. **Parent Involvement in Schooling**—Parent(s) are actively involved in helping young person succeed in school.
7. **Community Values Youth**—Young person perceives that adults in the community value youth.
8. **Youth as Resources**—Young people are given useful roles in the community.
9. **Service to Others**—Young person serves in the community one hour or more per week.
10. **Safety**—Young person feels safe at home, at school, and in the neighborhood.
11. **Family Boundaries**—Family has clear rules and consequences and monitors the young person's whereabouts.
12. **School Boundaries**—School provides clear rules and consequences.
13. **Neighborhood Boundaries**—Neighbors take responsibility for monitoring young people's behavior.
14. **Adult Role Models**—Parent(s) and other adults model positive, responsible behavior.
15. **Positive Peer Influence**—Young person's best friends model responsible behavior.
16. **High Expectations**—Both parent(s) and teachers encourage the young person to do well.
17. **Creative Activities**—Young person spends three or more hours per week in lessons or practice in music, theater, or other arts.
18. **Youth Programs**—Young person spends three or more hours per week in sports, clubs, or organizations at school and/or in the community.
19. **Religious Community**—Young person spends one or more hours per week in activities in a religious institution.

20. **Time at Home**—Young person is out with friends "with nothing special to do" two or fewer nights per week.
21. **Achievement Motivation**—Young person is motivated to do well in school.
22. **School Engagement**—Young person is actively engaged in learning.
23. **Homework**—Young person reports doing at least one hour of homework every school day.
24. **Bonding to School**—Young person cares about her or his school.
25. **Reading for Pleasure**—Young person reads for pleasure three or more hours per week.
26. **Caring**—Young person places high value on helping other people.
27. **Equality and Social Justice**—Young person places high value on promoting equality and reducing hunger and poverty.
28. **Integrity**—Young person acts on convictions and stands up for her or his beliefs.
29. **Honesty**—Young person "tells the truth even when it is not easy."
30. **Responsibility**—Young person accepts and takes personal responsibility.
31. **Restraint**—Young person believes it is important not to be sexually active or to use alcohol or other drugs.
32. **Planning and Decision Making**—Young person knows how to plan ahead and make choices.
33. **Interpersonal Competence**—Young person has empathy, sensitivity, and friendship skills.
34. **Cultural Competence**—Young person has knowledge of and comfort with people of different cultural/racial/ethnic backgrounds.
35. **Resistance Skills**—Young person can resist negative peer pressure and dangerous situations.
36. **Peaceful Conflict Resolution**—Young person seeks to resolve conflict nonviolently.
37. **Personal Power**—Young person feels he or she has control over "things that happen to me."
38. **Self-Esteem**—Young person reports having a high self-esteem.
39. **Sense of Purpose**—Young person reports that "my life has a purpose."
40. **Positive View of Personal Future**—Young person is optimistic about her or his personal future.

Community Cafeteria

Focus: Youth identify opportunities for involvement in their community.

Activity: Explain that one way a community shows how it values young people is by offering activities for them to get involved in. Mention several types of activities that communities offer (possibilities include sports, arts, religious programs, hobbies, social action, service, educational enrichment, and business) and then ask youth to form eight teams according to types of activities they're most interested in. Tell team members they should work together to identify organizations and clubs in the community that offer activities in their chosen area. They can find this information through the community newspaper, chamber of commerce, city hall, their school counselor's office, the library, and community education offices. Depending on how much time you have, you may have to use two group sessions to complete the activity—youth could conduct research during the first session and follow through with the bonus idea (following the discussion questions) during the second session. Another option is to have young people spend one session visiting your city hall, the library, or school and gathering information before getting together again to present their findings to the group.

Once teams finish, have them report what they found to the larger group. Write each team's findings on the chalkboard or newsprint.

Discussion Questions:

• *What types of activities are most available for youth your age? Where are the gaps?*

• *Were you surprised by what you found?*

• *Overall, by what you see offered to youth, how much do you think the community values youth? Why?*

• *Which community organizations seem to value youth most? Which don't value youth much at all? Why do you think this is so?*

Bonus Idea: Depending on how much information youth gather, they may want to host an activity fair for other youth to attend and learn how they can get involved in their communities. The youth group members could also write an article for a school newspaper.

2
Breaking the Ice

Young people often find themselves in situations where they don't know each other. When young people are given opportunities to learn each other's names and slowly begin to build relationships, they're more likely to work together. Whether you're in a school, organization, or some other setting, you can use the activities in this chapter to help young people get to know each other and build a strong sense of community.

20 | Bouncing Questions

Focus: Youth get to know each other by asking questions.

Developmental Assets Tie-in:

33—Interpersonal Competence
38—Self-Esteem

You will need:

• a chair for each young person

• a ball that bounces (such as a rubber ball or ping pong ball)

Activity: Have young people form a circle with the chairs in the room, then ask them to sit in the circle while you explain the activity. You're going to say one person's name, ask a question, and bounce a ball toward that person. That person will then answer the question.

Questions could include:
• Which after-school activity do you enjoy best?

• Who supports you most?

• Which school subject is most interesting to you?

• Who is in your family?

If youth don't know each other well and aren't outgoing, choose one question that each person should answer. After a while, switch to another question. That way young people can focus on learning each other's names instead of having to learn someone's name and come up with a question.

Once one young person has answered the question, he or she then says another person's name in the circle, asks a question, and bounces the ball toward that person. Keep doing this until everyone has had multiple turns.

Discussion Questions:

• Is it easy or hard to learn people's names? Why?

• How often do you find yourself in situations where you don't know people's names? What do you do?

• How does it feel when people use your name when they talk to you?

• Why is it important to learn people's names?

21 | The Best of the Best

Focus: Youth reveal their favorite classes and teachers.

Developmental Assets Tie-in:

5—Caring School Climate
22—School Engagement

Activity: Have youth stand throughout the room. Begin by asking each person to name a favorite school subject; then have everyone create groups according to that subject. For example, have all those who said "math" gather together. Ask someone from each group to explain why he or she likes that subject, then ask youth why they think some subjects become favored more than others.

Have the larger group stand throughout the room again. Ask everyone to name their favorite teachers. (If you are a teacher, suggest that youth should not name you, even if you are one of their favorites.) Again, have youth create groups according to the person named.

After that, ask youth to name the best class they have ever taken.

Discussion Questions:

• What qualities do good teachers have?

• How does a good teacher make learning interesting and fun?

• What is/was so great about your favorite class?

• What is it about learning that is most exciting to you?

• How can you get excited about learning when the subject or teaching method seems boring?

Ideal School Boundaries

Developmental Assets Tie-in:

12—School Boundaries
29—Honesty
31—Restraint

Imagine yourself as the one who makes all the final decisions about the rules and consequences at your school. Write what you think would be a fair and clear rule and consequence for each of the areas below. Pair up with another person to compare your ideas and discuss what seems fair.

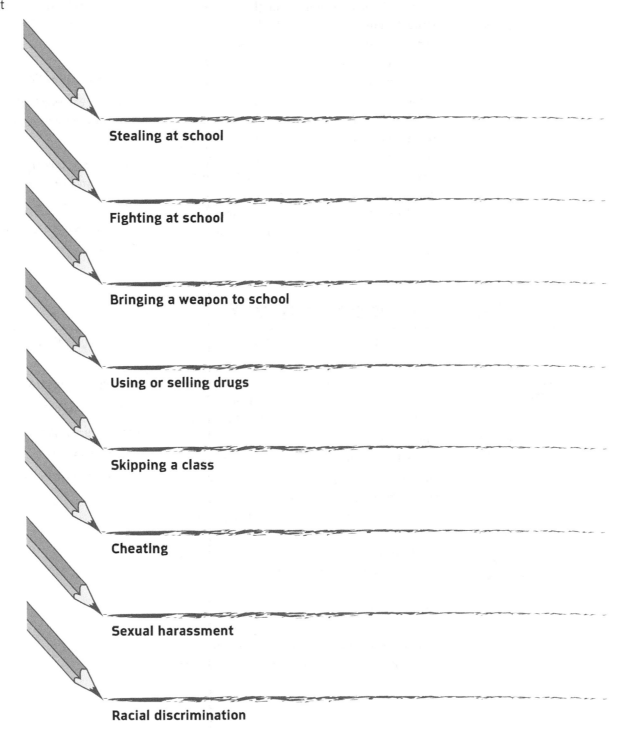

Stealing at school

Fighting at school

Bringing a weapon to school

Using or selling drugs

Skipping a class

Cheating

Sexual harassment

Racial discrimination

23 | Where's the Common Ground?

Focus: Youth discover what members of their group have in common.

Developmental Assets Tie-in:

5—Caring School Climate
24—Bonding to School

You will need:

• pencils or pens

• writing paper

Activity: Ask youth to line up according to age, then pair the first person in line with the last person in line, and so on. Ask the pairs to list what they have in common—everything from the mundane to the important. (If pairs are struggling to get started on this list, suggest comparing notes on things like favorite color, favorite ice cream, the last good movie they saw.)

After a few minutes, have pairs form teams of four. Each pair should read its list to its new team, and then the whole team should look for things that appear on both lists. Teams should create a new list of things their team of four has in common, adding other items they may discover.

After a few minutes, have teams merge to become teams of eight. Each original team of four should read its list to the new team of eight, and then they should all compile a new list of things that everyone on the team has in common, adding any other items they may come up with.

Finally, call everyone together and compare lists so everyone can learn what the entire group has in common.

Discussion Questions:

• *What items on this list surprise you? If you were to do this activity with your entire school, what items might be on the list?*

• *Would knowing about the things you have in common with other youth influence your feelings about your school? Why or why not?*

• *Is a sense of common ground important to you? Why or why not?*

24 | Getting to Know You

Focus: Youth identify what they have in common with each other.

Developmental Assets Tie-in:

33—Interpersonal Competence
38—Self-Esteem

You will need:

• a piece of paper for each young person

• a marker for each young person

Activity: Give each young person a piece of paper and a marker. Ask youth to write their names at the top of the paper and to number their paper from 1 to 10.

Ask everyone to make a list of 10 things they enjoy doing. Examples could include playing soccer, reading, playing video games, eating, playing a musical instrument, or talking on the phone.

Once everyone has finished, have them form pairs to compare lists. Tell them they should sign their name next to every common item on their partner's paper.

Then yell, "Switch!" Have young people find another partner to compare their lists with and to repeat the activity. Do this a number of times.

Discussion Questions:

• *What did you discover during this activity?*

• *What do you have in common with a lot of people? What is unique to you?*

• *Why is it important to see what we have in common?*

| # Model Photo Album

**Developmental
Assets Tie-in:**

15—Positive
Peer Influence
33—Interpersonal
Competence

Choose two friends you really look up to. Place photographs of these two friends in the places designated below. If you don't have a photograph, consider taking one with an instant camera, drawing a picture, or just writing the name of your friend in the picture frame. Under each picture, write which attributes you particularly like and admire about each friend.

Traits I admire about _____

_____

_____

_____

_____

Traits I admire about _____

_____

_____

_____

_____

26 | Safe—or Not?

Focus: Youth take a stand on safety in various aspects of their lives.

Developmental Assets Tie-in:

10—Safety
28—Integrity

You will need:

• a piece of rope or masking tape

Note:

This activity may remind students of negative experiences (for example, an abusive home environment, school incident, or act of violence). If you are concerned about your ability to deal with students' feelings about such situations, check in before the activity with a school guidance counselor, social worker, or someone else who has experience in this area.

Activity: Before you do this activity, designate one area to be home base and another area as a tightrope. Either lay a piece of rope on the floor or use masking tape to symbolize a rope.

Have everyone stand. Make sure there is enough room for youth to move from one area to another. Explain that you're going to name various aspects of their lives, one at a time. If youth always feel safe in that place, they should move to home base. If they sometimes don't feel safe in that place, they should stand on the tightrope, where they should try to balance.

• their neighborhood
• their school
• a congregation
• a nearby rural community
• shops
• your state
• youth hangouts
• a nearby suburb
• after-school activities
• home
• the closest city at 1 a.m. on a weekend
• the world

Give youth time to scan the room and observe how their classmates answered before you name the next place.

Discussion Questions:

• *Where do you feel the safest? Why?*

• *Where do you feel least safe? Why?*

• *Why is it important to feel safe?*

• *What affects how safe you feel? (For example, being alone or being in a group.)*

• *What suggestions do you have to make some of the unsafe places in your life safer?*

27 | It's Puzzling

Focus: Youth work together to solve a puzzle.

Developmental Assets Tie-in:

27—Equality and Social Justice
32—Planning and Decision Making
33—Interpersonal Competence

You will need:

• two 24-piece puzzles

Activity: Before you do this activity, hide the box for one of the puzzles so youth cannot see the picture on the front. Keep it available for the end of the activity.

Form two groups. Give one group a 24-piece puzzle without the picture. Give the other group a 24-piece puzzle with the picture. Have groups start working on their puzzles at the same time. See which group finishes first.

Discussion Questions:

• *Was this competition fair? Why or why not?*

• *What other competitions in life are like this one?*

• *What's it like to work together when you know what you're doing? What if you don't know what you're doing?*

• *Why does it help to see where you're going when you're working as a group?*

Creative Circles

When someone says it's time for a "creative activity," do you find a way to leave the room? Play this game with someone to consider how creativity is part of your life and your community each day.

Use coins as game pieces (one per person). You also will need one die. After you roll the die, move to a circle with that number. The number must be connected with your current place by a line. When you land on a new circle, you must be able to name one place in your community where you can do the activity mentioned or else go back to your previous place. If there is no connecting circle with the number you roll, you lose your turn. First player to the top wins.

Developmental Assets Tie-in:

17—Creative Activities

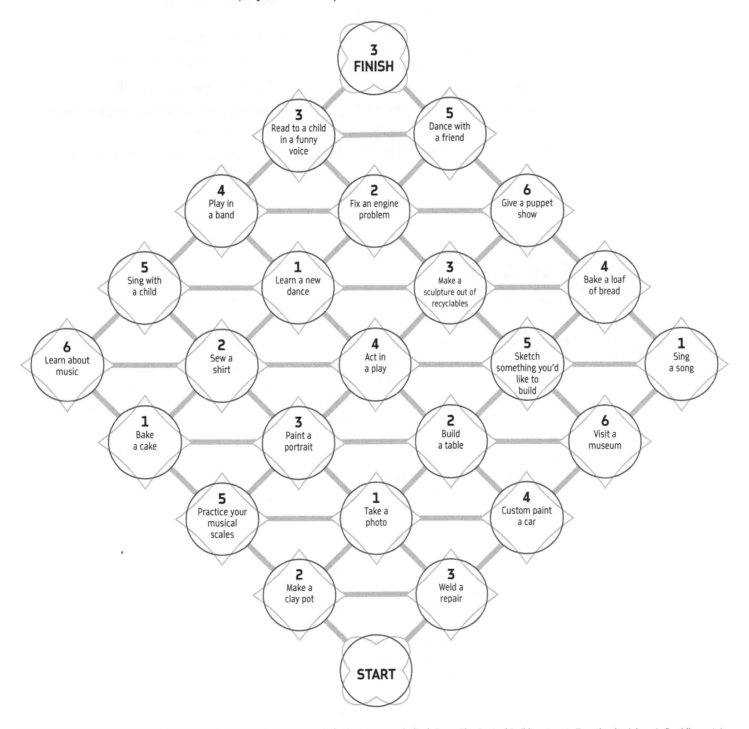

29 | Near and Far

Focus: Youth get to know each other.

Developmental Assets Tie-in:

33—Interpersonal Competence

You will need:

• Masking tape (or painter's tape)

Activity: Mark a long line on the floor with masking or painter's tape.

Have young people spread throughout the room. Explain that the line on the floor represents a continuum. Tell them that you're going to ask them a question and that they should move onto the portion of the line that best fits their answer to the question. Designate which end of the tape represents the two extremes of each question so that young people know where to line up. They will need to talk with each other to figure out where they should stand.

Ask questions, such as these, one at a time:
• Who lives farthest from or closest to school?

• Who has a birthday in early January or late December?

• Who is the oldest child or youngest child in their family?

• Who has lived in this community the shortest or the longest?

• Who woke up the earliest this morning—or the latest?

Give young people time to talk about what they're learning about themselves and each other after each question.

Discussion Questions:
• *What did you learn about yourself?*

• *What did you learn about each other?*

• *What do you find out when you take the time to talk with someone else?*

• *How can we get to know each other even better?*

30 | Say What?

Focus: Youth get to know each other while using their imagination.

Developmental Assets Tie-in:

15—Positive Peer Influence
33—Interpersonal Competence

Activity: Have young people sit in a circle. Explain that you're going to do a get-to-know-you activity. You're going to go around the circle, and one person at a time, ask a question that each youth should "answer" by showing an action for everyone to mimic. Make sure each youth tells the group his or her name before you ask the question. Some examples of questions include:
• Which expression would you make to show you're bored?

• What kind of face would you make if you were totally disgusted?

• What do you wish people would do more often to show others that they cared?

• What really bugs you?

• What's your favorite weekend activity?

• If you could invent a new gesture, what would it look like?

Discussion Questions:
• *Is it harder to be silly or serious? Why?*

• *When you're learning someone's name, is it better to just be introduced or to learn a bit more about the person? Why?*

• *How easy or hard does our society make it to get to know people? Why?*

• *What are good discussion starters when you're meeting someone new?*

31 | All About Me

Write your first and last name vertically on this page. Then write one word or phrase for each letter of your name. (Feel free to use a dictionary or thesaurus for ideas.)

Developmental Assets Tie-in:

33—Interpersonal Competence
37—Personal Power
38—Self-Esteem
40—Positive View of Personal Future

For example: Liza Bandt might write:

L: Loves to sing
 I: Idealistic
Z: Zany
A: Artistic

B: Bashful
A: Animal lover
N: Nutty
D: Determined
T: Thorough

3
Raising
Self-Awareness

Growing up includes developing a set of personal

attitudes that help young people thrive as

independent, competent individuals. These

attitudes shape the way young people look at

themselves, the world, and their future, and

help them succeed in the challenges they face.

Activities for helping young people view their own

sense of power, purpose, worth, and promise are

included in this chapter.

32 | Wall of Support

Focus: Youth identify all the ways people support them.

Developmental Assets Tie-in:

1—Family Support
3—Other Adult Relationships
4—Caring Neighborhood
5—Caring School Climate

You will need:

• a large sheet of newsprint or other type of paper

• markers, paint, or other colorful drawing supplies

• masking tape

Activity: Hang a large piece of newsprint or other type of paper on the wall. Title it "Ways Others Support Us." Have youth think of all the ways individuals show them love and support. As they think of ideas, have them write or draw pictures of the ideas on the paper. Encourage them to be creative and make the paper look like a graffiti wall. If you can, display the graffiti wall after you've completed the activity.

Discussion Questions:

• *What are the most common ways individuals show their support? What are some unusual ways?*

• *What were some times in your life when these kinds of support were particularly important? How did they make a difference?*

• *Some people don't experience as much support as others. How can young people encourage people to provide more support? (Note to facilitators: Be aware that for some young people, asking for more support is difficult. Help young people think of creative, safe ways to find support.)*

• *How can youth support each other?*

Bonus Idea: If several groups are doing this activity at the same time, consider hanging all the sheets of paper together in a long hallway, cafeteria, or other common space for youth and adults throughout the building to see.

33 | Gift Chain

Focus: Youth display the strengths and resources they offer.

Developmental Assets Tie-in:

37—Personal Power
38—Self-Esteem
39—Sense of Purpose
40—Positive View of Personal Future

You will need:

• construction paper in a variety of colors

• pens in a variety of colors

• scissors

• tape

• thin cardboard or poster board

Activity: Make several cardboard patterns of a person with outstretched arms. Make the figure at least eight inches tall. You may be able to use a gingerbread cookie cutter as a guide for the pattern.

As you begin, ask, "Is it easier to tell other people about your strengths or about your weaknesses? Why is that?"

Explain that this activity is an opportunity for youth to take pride in their own strengths and to learn more about the strengths of others in the group. Ask each person to choose a color of construction paper and cut out an outline, using the patterns you've provided. Instruct them to write this phrase on one side of the figure: "My strengths are . . ." and then to list three strengths. On the back of the figure, they can write their names and add any artistic touches that they desire.

Gather in a circle and ask each youth to share what he or she listed as personal strengths. Affirm each person. Pass tape around the circle, having youth tape their cutout figures together at the hands. Hang this chain of "strong people" in your meeting space.

Discussion Questions:

• *What did you discover during this activity?*

• *Why is it important to be aware of your own strengths?*

• *How can we encourage each other to use our strengths and gifts?*

• *How might our community be different if everyone acted on her or his strengths?*

Developmental Assets Tie-in:

17—Creative Activities
21—Achievement Motivation

One of the aspects of strong arts programs is that they open you up to being creative. Teresa Amabile, Ph.D., author of *Growing Up Creative* (Creative Education Foundation, 1989), has identified several traits of creative people. Check each of the traits below that you currently have and star the ones you want to work on.

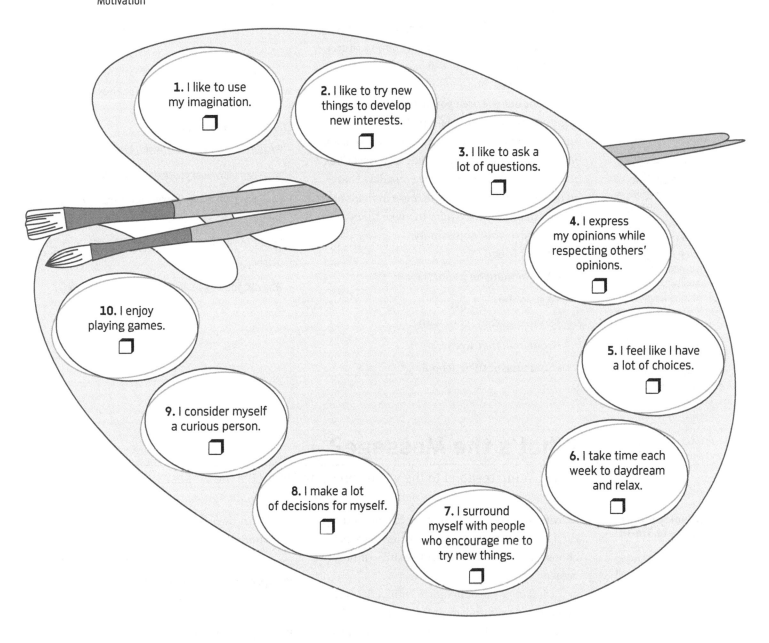

1. I like to use my imagination.

2. I like to try new things to develop new interests.

3. I like to ask a lot of questions.

4. I express my opinions while respecting others' opinions.

5. I feel like I have a lot of choices.

6. I take time each week to daydream and relax.

7. I surround myself with people who encourage me to try new things.

8. I make a lot of decisions for myself.

9. I consider myself a curious person.

10. I enjoy playing games.

35 | How Safe Do You Feel?

Focus: Youth express their feelings about safety.

Developmental Assets Tie-in:

10—Safety

You will need:

• markers

• newsprint

• tape (or an easel)

Note:

This activity may remind students of negative experiences (for example, an abusive home environment, school incident, or act of violence). If you are concerned about your ability to deal with students' feelings about such situations, check in before the activity with a school guidance counselor, social worker, or someone else who has experience in this area.

Activity: Write each of these phrases on a separate sheet of newsprint: "Completely Safe" and "Not Safe at All." Clear a long space in your meeting area and hang one chart at each end of the space.

Ask youth what people mean when they say someone is or is not safe. Record their criteria for determining who is "safe" and who is "not safe" on newsprint.

Point out the area you have cleared and the charts at each end. Explain that this is a continuum, and as you name a person, youth should move to the place along the line that describes the degree to which he or she considers that person safe or unsafe. Name these individuals, adding details as necessary to make them more applicable to your community:

• A best friend
• A teammate on a sports team
• A neighbor
• Someone they work with
• Someone they live with
• Someone at their school
• Someone who lives in their community
• A stranger
• A celebrity
• A teacher
• Someone who has been convicted of a crime
• A police officer

After each item, ask for volunteers to tell why they chose to stand where they did.

Discussion Questions:

• *What determines how safe or unsafe a person is?*

• *What can individual youth do to be safe?*

• *What can community leaders do to make a community safer?*

• *What can young people do to be safe with an unsafe person?*

• *Who can you talk to about individuals and safety?*

36 | What's the Message?

Focus: Youth respond to the values presented in media messages.

Developmental Assets Tie-in:

26—Caring
27—Equality and Social Justice
28—Integrity
29—Honesty
30—Responsibility
31—Restraint

You will need:

• several magazines popular with youth

• markers

Activity: Ask youth to form pairs for this activity, then give each pair some magazines. Have pairs choose five ads that represent positive or negative values.

Challenge participants to think critically about the words and graphic images in each ad in order to describe the message they are receiving from it. Have pairs write on the ad the message that they are receiving. Coach them with questions such as:

• What action does the advertiser want you to take?

• What does the advertiser want you to feel about yourself?

• What does the advertiser want you to feel about others?

Ask each pair to present their ads to the group, explaining their reasons for the message they wrote on each one.

Discussion Questions:

Spread all the ads on the floor or table in the center of your group. Ask:

• *Which ads promote values that are important to you or your family?*

• *Which ads promise to improve something about you?*

• *Which ads promote positive ways to spend your time or money in order to build your self-esteem?*

Developmental Assets Tie-in:

21—Achievement Motivation
22—School Engagement
23—Homework

Great news! For your birthday you received a gift card to Everything Electronics, and it's enough to buy that new MP3 player you've been wanting. The way you approach this happy task can tell you a lot about how you learn. Choose just one answer for each of the questions below and see what you discover!

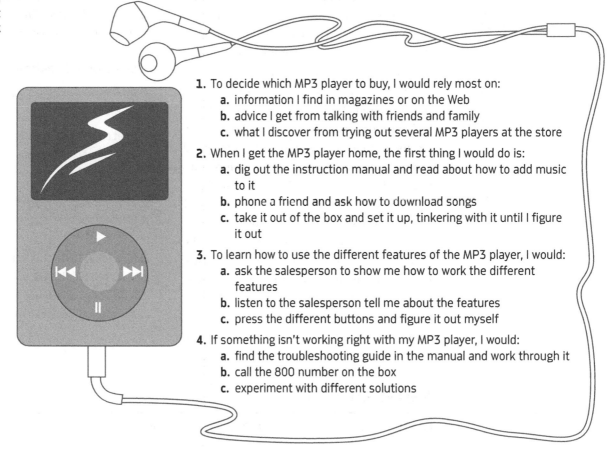

1. To decide which MP3 player to buy, I would rely most on:
   a. information I find in magazines or on the Web
   b. advice I get from talking with friends and family
   c. what I discover from trying out several MP3 players at the store

2. When I get the MP3 player home, the first thing I would do is:
   a. dig out the instruction manual and read about how to add music to it
   b. phone a friend and ask how to download songs
   c. take it out of the box and set it up, tinkering with it until I figure it out

3. To learn how to use the different features of the MP3 player, I would:
   a. ask the salesperson to show me how to work the different features
   b. listen to the salesperson tell me about the features
   c. press the different buttons and figure it out myself

4. If something isn't working right with my MP3 player, I would:
   a. find the troubleshooting guide in the manual and work through it
   b. call the 800 number on the box
   c. experiment with different solutions

If most of your answers are "a," you probably tend to be a **visual learner**. You enjoy reading and it's easy for you to learn from written descriptions, instructions, and charts or graphs. You may like to color-code things as you organize them. When someone demonstrates how to do something, you can then do it yourself.

If most of your answers are "b," you probably tend to be an **auditory learner**. You enjoy discussing information and it's easy for you to learn from conversations with others. You may like to "talk things out" to find the solution to a problem. When someone tells you how to do something, you can then do it yourself.

If most of your answers are "c," you probably tend to be a **kinesthetic learner**. You enjoy being active and moving, and it's easy for you to learn new things by doing hands-on experiments and projects. You may like to draw diagrams or pictures as notes to help you remember information. When you figure out how to do something by trial and error, you can remember how to do it again.

Did you discover that you have some characteristics of each learning style? This is normal, because you have been exposed to many ways of learning in school. Most people, however, have one style that is dominant. How could you use this information about your learning style to help with your schoolwork?

38 | This Makes Me Mad!

Focus: Youth imagine peaceful solutions to situations that anger them.

Developmental Assets Tie-in:

33—Interpersonal Competence
36—Peaceful Conflict Resolution

You will need:

• pencils or pens

• writing paper

Activity: Distribute paper and pencils. Ask each youth to think about a situation in daily life that makes her or him mad, then write this situation on paper (for example, missing the bus, getting a low score on a test, being teased). Explain to youth that they will be sharing the situation with the group, so they should write something they will feel comfortable discussing.

When everyone has finished writing, ask youth to circulate with their sheets of paper, look for other youth who wrote something similar, and form a team with them. (If some youth cannot find anyone with a similar complaint, ask them to form an "Assorted Gripes" team.)

Ask each team to write "What has helped" and "What has not helped" on one of their sheets and to take notes while they discuss how they have tried to deal with their shared gripe. Have each team prepare a report to the group that offers advice on what to try and what not to try when others face this type of situation. As teams give their reports, look for further points

of discussion. For example, if one group writes "Trying to reason with the person" under "What has not helped" because this method didn't work once with a certain individual, explain that even good, healthy ideas fail to work sometimes and it is worth it to make another attempt.

Discussion Questions:

• *Did these shared gripes have anything in common? If so, what?*

• *What did the "What has helped" advice have in common? What did the "What has not helped" advice have in common?*

• *What is one new thing you will try in a situation that makes you angry?*

Bonus Idea: Redo this activity and call it "This Makes Me Glad!" Ask youth to think about the things they experience that make them happy or encourage them to keep a positive attitude.

39 | Rare Gems

Focus: Youth talk about what makes them unique.

Developmental Assets Tie-in:

37—Personal Power
38—Self-Esteem
39—Sense of Purpose
40—Positive View of Personal Future

Activity: Have youth find a partner. Ask partners to tell each other one surprising fact about themselves. For example, someone might say she was born premature, weighing only two pounds, and another person might say he is fluent in a second language.

After partners have talked, have young people find new partners. This time, have partners tell each other about the most interesting place they have ever visited.

Give young people time to talk. Occasionally have them switch partners to discuss a topic, such as these:

• Where are your ancestors from?

• What unusual food do you like?

• What is your favorite holiday? Why?

• What is the funniest movie or TV show you've ever seen? Funniest book you've ever read?

• If you were a rare gem, which gem would you be? Why?

Discussion Questions:

• *What did you discover about yourself by talking with a partner?*

• *How does telling someone about yourself affect how you see yourself?*

• *How do other people help you figure out who you are?*

• *What can we do to become the best people we can be?*

40 | Your Favorite Books

Developmental Assets Tie-in:

25—Reading for Pleasure

You can gain a lot from reading books. Sometimes a book can serve as fun summer reading; other times it goes beyond entertainment and teaches you something—maybe about the history of another culture, how a plane works, how other teens—fictional or real—have coped with puberty, or just how the last *Harry Potter* ends. Books offer a whole world you can explore!

Think about the three best books you've ever read. Write their titles in the books below. Were they funny or sad? Did they help you see the world from a different perspective? Did they help you see yourself differently? Did they inspire you?

Now think of four books you would like to read in the near future and write their titles in the books below. Why are you interested in reading these books?

41 | My Spark

Focus: Youth identify what gets them excited and gives them meaning.

Developmental Assets Tie-in:

37—Personal Power
38—Self-Esteem
39—Sense of Purpose
40—Positive View of Personal Future

You will need:

• an unlit candle or small flashlight for youth to hold and pass

Activity: Have youth sit in a circle. Say that you're going to do an activity where everyone will take turns talking about their spark. Explain that a spark is an interest or talent a young person has that gets her or him excited and is something he or she enjoys doing. A spark can be started by playing a musical instrument, playing a sport, writing poetry, fixing a motorcycle, growing houseplants, and more.

Give one young person the unlit candle or flashlight. Have the person answer this question: What is my spark? If the person isn't sure, ask that person what he or she enjoys doing best during her or his free time. Then have the person pass the candle to the left. Have the next person answer the same question. Go around the circle until everyone has answered the question.

Repeat the activity with questions such as these:

• What keeps your spark going?
• What tries to put out your spark?
• Who supports your spark best?
• When do you have time to work on your spark?

Discussion Questions:

• *What did you discover about sparks through this activity?*
• *Why is it important to have a spark?*
• *What would our world look like if everyone followed her or his spark?*

42 | Where I Fit

Focus: Youth identify the different roles they have.

Developmental Assets Tie-in:

8—Youth as Resources
30—Responsibility
34—Cultural Competence

Activity: Have youth form a circle. Ask for three volunteers to leave the room.

Tell the young people in the circle that when you invite the volunteers back into the room, they will try to rejoin the circle. Tell the group to do whatever they can (without hurting anyone) to try to keep the three volunteers out.

Invite the three volunteers in and ask them to join the circle. After they have tried unsuccessfully, stop the activity. Then ask for three new volunteers. Have those volunteers leave the room. Incorporate the original group of volunteers into the large circle.

Tell the young people in the circle that when you invite the three volunteers back to the room, this time they should let them easily join the circle.

Invite the three volunteers in. Ask the three volunteers to join the circle. Don't be surprised if the volunteers try to use force at first, assuming they won't be let in.

Discussion Questions:

• *What was it like to keep people out of the circle?*
• *When have you experienced places or situations where you didn't feel like you fit in?*
• *What was it like to let people enter the circle easily?*
• *When have you experienced places or situations where you fit in right away?*
• *Why is it important to fit in?*
• *How can we help others fit in more easily?*

Think about what you like about yourself. Then read the words below and circle the ones that describe you. (Don't be shy! Circle as many words as you want.) Add your own words if you feel some are missing.

Developmental Assets Tie-in:

38—Self-Esteem

Practical   Active   Laid-back   **Driven**

Thoughtful   **Enterprising**   Independent

Helpful   Patient   Musical   Healthy

Resourceful   Social   Ethical

Hard-working   Responsive   **Funny**

Talkative   Quiet   Sympathetic   Quick

Friendly   Responsible   Inquisitive

Open-minded   Patriotic   **Moral**

Carefree   Relaxed   Imaginative

Honest   Stimulating   **HAPPY**   Kind

Flexible   INVESTIGATIVE

Intelligent   Proud

Sensitive   Understanding

Decisive   DEPENDABLE   **Determined**

Silly   Predictable   Loving   Jovial

Creative   **Direct**   Adventurous   **Leader**

44 | No, Not Me

Focus: Youth identify the values and reasons that explain why they would never do certain things.

Activity: After youth form pairs, tell them they're going to have a contest to see who can name the most things they would never do; for example, "I would never cheat on a test" or "I would never go bungee jumping."

Explain the rules to the group:
- The things they would never do have to be possible,
- They can't repeat what their partner has already said, and
- They have to alternate between silly and serious topics.

Have pairs begin. After about 10 minutes, stop the activity.

Discussion Questions:

- *What are the silly things people said they wouldn't do?*
- *What are the serious things? (If no one mentions anything related to sexual activity or the use of alcohol or other drugs, ask if anyone mentioned these things in their discussions.)*
- *What reasons explain why you decided not to do some of the serious things? (If youth need prompting, mention safety, parents' wishes, personal values, laws, religious beliefs.)*
- *In what ways do youth support or pressure each other in these areas?*
- *What are some ways to respond to negative pressures?*

My Idea: *"I link this idea to turtles and wasps. I talk about the dangers of wasps and how wasps move fast and may actually sting each other. On the other hand, turtles appear slow in making decisions, but they usually live a lot longer and get along much better. So I ask: Which group do you want to hang with?"*

—James Robinson, Bowling Green, Kentucky

45 | Symbols for Me

Focus: Youth describe how a symbol represents who they are.

You will need:

- index cards (one per person)
- a holder for the cards (small box, envelope, bowl, etc.)
- pen or pencil for each young person

Activity: Give each young person an index card and a pen or pencil. Ask youth to write the name of one object that describes or symbolizes who they are. Examples might include a rock, a diamond, a rubber band, and so on. Collect those cards and place them in the container.

Have youth sit in a circle and take turns drawing one symbol. Make sure that every person has a card that is different from the one he or she originally wrote.

Start with one person who explains how he or she is like the object written on the card. Go around the circle until everyone has done this.

Then repeat the activity. This time, have youth explain how they are like the original object they wrote on their card before it was collected. (This will be a different object.)

Discussion Questions:

- *Is it easy or hard to describe yourself like an object? Why?*
- *What did you discover about yourself when you tried to describe yourself with an object that you didn't choose?*
- *Why do some people use symbols to describe things?*
- *How can a symbol inspire us to be better people?*
- *How else can we talk about who we are?*

46 | Stressed Out!

Developmental Assets Tie-in:

37—Personal Power
38—Self-Esteem
39—Sense of Purpose
40—Positive View of Personal Future

As a baby, you probably cried when you felt scared, crabby, or anxious. Now that you're older, there are other ways for you to express feelings such as fear, anxiety, embarrassment, anger, or stress. Your palms might sweat, your heart might race, your face might get red, or you might feel sick to your stomach—these are all signals or inner cues that are triggered when you feel a certain emotion. Child psychiatrist Dr. Bruce Perry has studied how we respond to these brain messages and body signals. He explains that as a person matures, it is easier for him or her to stop and think before acting on raw emotion. The bottom line? It's really up to you to decide how you choose to react in certain situations.

Think about the things that stress you out (some examples are listed below). What are some positive ways to handle stress? Describe them below.

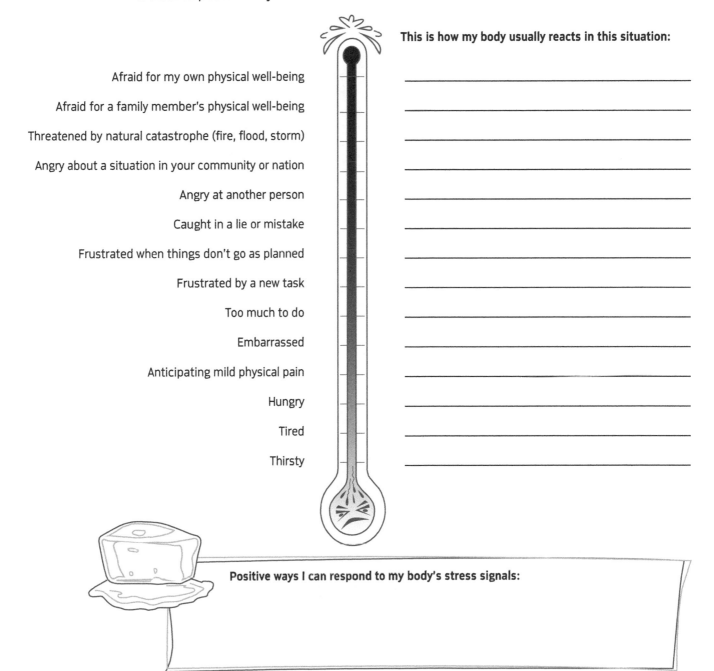

This is how my body usually reacts in this situation:

Afraid for my own physical well-being

Afraid for a family member's physical well-being

Threatened by natural catastrophe (fire, flood, storm)

Angry about a situation in your community or nation

Angry at another person

Caught in a lie or mistake

Frustrated when things don't go as planned

Frustrated by a new task

Too much to do

Embarrassed

Anticipating mild physical pain

Hungry

Tired

Thirsty

Positive ways I can respond to my body's stress signals:

4
Building Skills

To negotiate the maze of choices and options,

young people need skills that they can

master and use. Skills lay the foundation for

independence and competence that youth need

as they become adults. This chapter offers ideas

for building essential skills that all young people

need to succeed.

47	# Homework Centers

Focus: Youth imagine and design an ideal study area for their homes.

Developmental Assets Tie-in:

21—Achievement Motivation
23—Homework

You will need:

• a large sheet of newsprint or other paper—one for each group of three young people

• markers

Activity: Ask youth to form teams of three according to their favorite meal of the day (i.e., each team will consist of one person who likes breakfast, one who likes lunch, and one who likes dinner). Give each threesome a piece of paper and some markers, then ask each team to draw their ideal study area. Encourage youth to be creative and include such details as types of furniture and illustrations of how people are behaving.

After teams finish, have them hang their pictures on the wall and explain why they included the items that they did.

Discussion Questions:

• *What things did you identify for an ideal study place?*

• *Why is it important to have a specific area for doing homework?*

• *How many of these things are available to you right now?*

• *What else do you wish you had in your study area? Why?*

48	# Expanding Your World

Focus: Youth consider books that highlight characters of various ethnicities.

Developmental Assets Tie-in:

25—Reading for Pleasure
34—Cultural Competence
39—Sense of Purpose

You will need:

• a visiting librarian

Activity: Invite a librarian to meet with your group. Tell the librarian it would be ideal to bring novels that show protagonists of various ethnicities struggling to figure out their identities. Some helpful books include:

• *Sees Behind Trees* by Michael Dorris (Native American)

• *Finding My Voice* by Marie G. Lee (Asian)

• *To Kill a Mockingbird* by Harper Lee (Caucasian)

• *Parrot in the Oven: Mi Vida* by Victor Martinez (Latino)

• *Souls of the North Wind* by Chrissy McVay (Inuit/Aboriginal)

• *The Watsons Go to Birmingham—1963* by Christopher Paul Curtis (African American)

Have young people get together with the librarian to discuss the books. Ask the librarian to explain why it's important to read stories about people who are like us and who are different from us.

Discussion Questions:

• *What books or topics did you find interesting that you had never considered before? Why?*

• *Why is it easy to read books that cover topics we're used to?*

• *What would happen if you read a book about a main character who is different from you? When have you read a book like this? What happened?*

• *How can books help us form our identity?*

49 | What's Your Friend Potential?

Developmental Assets Tie-in:

15—Positive Peer Influence
33—Interpersonal Competence

Do you make new friends easily? Do you feel you do a good job of keeping friends? This sheet lists skills and characteristics that help you make and keep friends. Take a few minutes to rate yourself on each one. When you're done, choose one or two skills you want to improve this month. Remember, you can help your friends build asset 15, Positive Peer Influence, by being a great friend.

I listen as much as I talk when I'm with my friends.

HARDLY EVER   SOME OF THE TIME   MOST OF THE TIME

I keep secrets.

HARDLY EVER   SOME OF THE TIME   MOST OF THE TIME

I suggest things to do that other people think are fun.

HARDLY EVER   SOME OF THE TIME   MOST OF THE TIME

I keep the promises I make.

HARDLY EVER   SOME OF THE TIME   MOST OF THE TIME

I refuse to repeat gossip or hurtful comments about others.

HARDLY EVER   SOME OF THE TIME   MOST OF THE TIME

I can disagree with someone without getting angry or resorting to name-calling.

HARDLY EVER   SOME OF THE TIME   MOST OF THE TIME

I can sense when my friends are angry, frustrated, or feeling left out—even if they don't say anything.

HARDLY EVER   SOME OF THE TIME   MOST OF THE TIME

I stand up for what I think is right, even if my friends do not agree.

HARDLY EVER   SOME OF THE TIME   MOST OF THE TIME

I apologize when I goof up.

HARDLY EVER   SOME OF THE TIME   MOST OF THE TIME

I encourage friends to do their best.

HARDLY EVER   SOME OF THE TIME   MOST OF THE TIME

I do "random acts of kindness" for friends and others.

HARDLY EVER   SOME OF THE TIME   MOST OF THE TIME

I reach out to people who seem lonely or disconnected.

HARDLY EVER   SOME OF THE TIME   MOST OF THE TIME

50 | Decision Road Map

Focus: Youth experience the advantages and drawbacks of getting help from others in making decisions.

Developmental Assets Tie-in:

32—Planning and Decision Making
39—Sense of Purpose

You will need:

• three road maps

• pens or pencils

Activity: Place three road maps in different parts of the room. Form three teams and have each team choose a home-base point and destination on the map.

Encourage teams to find as many different routes as possible to get from their home base to their destination. Keep track of how many routes they come up with. Ask youth to discuss why they like or dislike each route. Finally, have them settle on one route.

Discussion Questions:

• What decisions did your team make that helped you find lots of routes?

• Was it harder or easier to pick a route as a team than it would have been to do so by yourself? Is the route you picked better because more people were involved in the decision-making process?

• How do you make a final decision if you have two or three options that seem equally good?

• What can help you make wise decisions?

51 | The Power of Resistance

Focus: Youth identify various ways to resist peer pressure and dangerous situations.

Developmental Assets Tie-in:

35—Resistance Skills

You will need:

• pieces of candy

Activity: Ask for two volunteers. Have one volunteer be the "pressurer" and the other person be the one who gets pressured. Give the pressurer some candy. Tell the volunteer who is to be pressured to do everything in her or his power to resist taking or eating any of the candy. Have the rest of your group observe what happens.

Start the activity. Tell the pressurer to use verbal tactics (within reason) to get the person to take or eat some of the candy. Watch what happens.

After a brief while, stop the activity. Then ask for another volunteer. Have that volunteer help the person being pressured to resist that pressure. Start the activity again with the pressurer trying to get the person to eat the candy when he or she has a supportive person with her or him.

Discussion Questions:

• What did the person do to resist taking and eating the candy?

• What was most effective? Least effective? Why?

• Why is it important to ask for support when you feel you can't resist pressure by yourself?

• What types of pressure do you face as teenagers? Who pressures you?

• What do you do to resist these pressures?

Developmental Assets Tie-in:

35—Resistance Skills

Sometimes it's easy to get caught up in the moment. You intend to refrain from doing something and then you are pressured into doing it. To keep that from happening, write seven creative ways to say no. If you wish, share your ideas with friends.

1 _____

2 _____

3 _____

4 _____

5 _____

6 _____

7 _____

53 | Pointing Fingers

Focus: Youth name sources of good events and bad events.

Developmental Assets Tie-in:

37—Personal Power
40—Positive View of Personal Future

You will need:

• three sheets of newsprint

• a marker

Activity: Hang newsprint on different sides of the room. Label one "My responsibility; my fault"; another "Someone else's responsibility; someone else's fault"; and the third "Pure luck; pure chance." Clear the area between the sheets so that youth can freely and safely move among them.

Explain that you will name situations and that youth are to run to the newsprint that best describes the probable cause of the event. Name both positive and negative situations, giving youth time to move around.

Name sample situations such as these:

• You earn an A in history.

• You're not invited to a party.

• You run for student council and don't win.

• You win the lead in the school play.

• You study hard but still fail a test.

• Someone steals your bike.

• You earn a scholarship.

• Someone threatens you with a gun.

Gather youth together. Say: "Dr. Martin Seligman has done psychological research on personal power. He says it's important to take responsibility and correct our behavior when things go wrong because of our choices, and also to see that bad things can happen to us that are not our fault. When we fail, we need to realize that we all make mistakes and we're all learning. When bad things happen that are beyond our control, we need to recognize that we're in a difficult situation but that we are not 'at fault.' Seligman also says that when good things happen to us, it's good to interpret those events globally. For example, if you get an A in math, it's better to think that you're smart overall rather than just smart in math or that you got lucky. Also, Seligman says we will have a healthier self-concept if we are specific about our interpretation of negative events. For example, if someone you're dating breaks up with you, it's better to believe that one individual has chosen not to date you, rather than think that nobody likes you."

Discussion Questions:

• *When is it easier to feel you have control in life: when bad things happen or when good things happen? Why?*

• *How does society teach us to interpret positive events? Negative events?*

• *Do you think some people have more personal power than others? Why?*

• *In what ways can you have more personal power?*

54 | The Arts around You

Focus: Youth identify opportunities for tapping into their artistic interests.

Developmental Assets Tie-in:

17—Creative Activities
21—Achievement Motivation

Activity: Have youth choose one form of artistic expression they like best or are most interested in learning about (for example, music lessons, orchestra, painting, drawing, theater, dance, choir). Then have youth identify groups, training, or other opportunities within your community or school to learn more about that form of fine art. Encourage youth to look into how much time the activity requires, where lessons are offered, the cost of being involved in the activity, and whether they need a background in that form of art before they join certain programs. Have youth report to the group what they have found.

Discussion Questions:

• *In what ways are you already involved in the arts?*

• *What do you get out of your involvement?*

• *Why do you think it's considered an asset to spend three or more hours each week in music or other arts training or practice?*

• *Which form of artistic expression are you interested in pursuing? Why?*

Think about a time in the past when you found yourself involved in a major conflict. Write about that situation by answering the questions below.

Developmental Assets Tie-in:

28—Integrity
36—Peaceful Conflict Resolution

1. What was the conflict about?

2. What was your view of the situation?

3. What was the other person's view of the situation?

4. Did you resolve the conflict? Why or why not?

5. If you had this conflict now, what would you do differently? Why?

6. Which of the following peaceful conflict resolution skills would you like to strengthen? (Check all that apply and star the one you would like to work on first.)

   ❏ Listen more to the other person and understand that person's position.

   ❏ Take time to deal with my emotions rather than taking them out on the other person.

   ❏ Be clear about my needs and opinions by using "I" messages.

   ❏ Brainstorm lots of ideas to resolve the conflict.

   ❏ Improve my problem-solving skills.

   ❏ Expect gradual improvements with some setbacks, not sudden improvements.

   ❏ Be sincere.

   ❏ Care for the person even though we're in conflict.

Focus: Youth assemble time jars to experience time management principles.

Developmental Assets Tie-in:

20—Time at Home
32—Planning and Decision Making

You will need:

• one glass or plastic pint jar (no lid needed) for each youth

• one-half cup gravel for each youth, poured into a sandwich bag

• one-half cup sand for each youth, poured into a sandwich bag

• three large rocks that will all fit in the jar at the same time for each youth

• five smaller rocks that will fit in the jar along with the three big rocks for each youth

• newsprint for each youth

• markers for each youth

• paper or plastic to cover the tables

Activity: Write each of the eight asset categories (Support, Empowerment, Boundaries and Expectations, Constructive Use of Time, Commitment to Learning, Positive Values, Social Competencies, and Positive Identity) on separate sheets of paper and post them around the room for participants to refer to during the activity. Use paper or plastic to cover the tables to assist with cleanup at the end of the activity.

Ask youth to work in pairs. Give each pair a marker and a sheet of newsprint, then distribute the jars, rocks, gravel, and sand. Tell the group that the jars represent the amount of time they have in one Wednesday, and the rocks and sand represent things they need or want to do on that Wednesday.

Tell youth to think about the next Wednesday and decide what the big rocks might represent that day—the things that are absolutely essential for them to do. Tell them to write these priorities on their newsprint.

Ask youth to think about what the small rocks would represent next Wednesday—the things that are fairly important to do. Tell them to write these on the newsprint as well. Then, have them think about things that need to be done but don't have to be completed by next Wednesday. Tell them to write three of these things—represented by the gravel—on the newsprint. Finally, have them think about what things they would like to do if they have time next Wednesday—the sand. Have them write three of these things on the newsprint.

Encourage youth to organize their ideas using the eight asset categories that are posted around the room. Ask pairs to share with the group some of the things they have written on their newsprint.

Next, explain that all of us have things we really like to do, and then tell the youth to pour their sand into their jars. Now tell them to add the rest of their rocks and gravel. What happens? Challenge youth to figure out how to make it all fit into the jar. (If youth have trouble figuring out how to do this, suggest that they put the big rocks in first.)

Discussion Questions:

• *What did you learn about planning from this activity? (If no one mentions it, say that things will only fit if the big things go in first.)*

• *What responsibilities would your big rocks represent if you were doing a time jar for an entire week? Why are they the same or different?*

• *What are the smaller rocks that keep getting in the way of your big rocks?*

• *How can you act in ways that reflect your biggest, most important priorities?*

My Idea: *"Let students keep their large rock as a reminder of what is first."*
—Nancy Tellett-Royce, Minneapolis, Minnesota

Developmental Assets Tie-in:

32—Planning and Decision Making

Think about your day tomorrow. In the time slots below, describe how you expect to spend your day. Remember to include eating, sleeping, studying, attending classes, after-school activities, family time, friend time, personal time, and transition time. At the end of the day, compare your planned schedule with what you actually did. How did having a plan affect how you spent your time?

Day of the Week

	Plan	What I Actually Did
Midnight		
1 a.m.		
2 a.m.		
3 a.m.		
4 a.m.		
5 a.m.		
6 a.m.		
7 a.m.		
8 a.m.		
9 a.m.		
10 a.m.		
11 a.m.		
Noon		
1 p.m.		
2 p.m.		
3 p.m.		
4 p.m.		
5 p.m.		
6 p.m.		
7 p.m.		
8 p.m.		
9 p.m.		
10 p.m.		
11 p.m.		

58 | Brainstorm Clouds

Focus: Youth brainstorm ways to encourage themselves to do homework.

Developmental Assets Tie-in:

21—Achievement Motivation
23—Homework

You will need:

• chalkboard and chalk (or newsprint and a marker)

Activity: Draw a large cloud on a chalkboard or newsprint. Ask youth to brainstorm as many ideas as they can that would encourage them to do homework or would help make it easier for them to do homework. (Remind youth that the purpose is to give as many ideas as possible and that there are no bad ideas.)

Discussion Questions:

• *Which of the ideas do you like the most? The least? Why?*

• *If a friend asked you for help in figuring out how to do homework better, what advice would you give?*

• *How do you feel about the time you spend doing homework? Is it too much? Not enough? How's your concentration?*

• *What motivates you to do homework?*

• *What keeps you from doing homework?*

59 | What Do You Do When You're Upset?

Focus: Youth explore different ways they process pain and emotion.

Developmental Assets Tie-in:

33—Interpersonal Competence
35—Resistance Skills
36—Peaceful Conflict Resolution

You will need:

• three pieces of newsprint

• masking or painter's tape

• markers (one for each young person)

• whistle (or some other sound maker, such as a kazoo)

Activity: Hang up the three pieces of newsprint in three different areas of the room. Label one "Helpful People," one "Helpful Activities," and one "Destructive Activities."

Create three groups. Station each group at each piece of newsprint.

Announce that the purpose of this activity is to examine how people deal with something that has upset them. Explain that when you say "go," groups are to write on the newsprint as many coping strategies as possible. For example, under "Helpful Activities," young people might write "journal," "talk to someone," or "exercise," and under "Helpful People," they might write "my best friend," "my mom," or "my favorite teacher."

Give each group two minutes at each piece of newsprint, then blow the whistle and have groups move to the newsprint on their right. Do the activity two more times so each group has an opportunity to write ideas on each piece of newsprint.

Discussion Questions:

• *What did you discover about the way people act when they get upset?*

• *What does our society promote: helpful behaviors or destructive behaviors? Why?*

• *Why does it matter how we behave when we're upset?*

• *How can we choose helpful ways to deal with situations when we're upset?*

Developmental Assets Tie-in:

8—Youth as Resources
9—Service to Others
30—Responsibility

Which responsibilities do you have at home? Do you clean your room? Take out the garbage? Empty the dishwasher? What about your school responsibilities? Do you do your homework? Take notes in class? Get to know your teachers? What about your community? Do you pick up litter? Enjoy the bike and walking trails? Voice your opinion about community matters? In the three spaces below, write one to three ways you do your part at home, at school, and in your community.

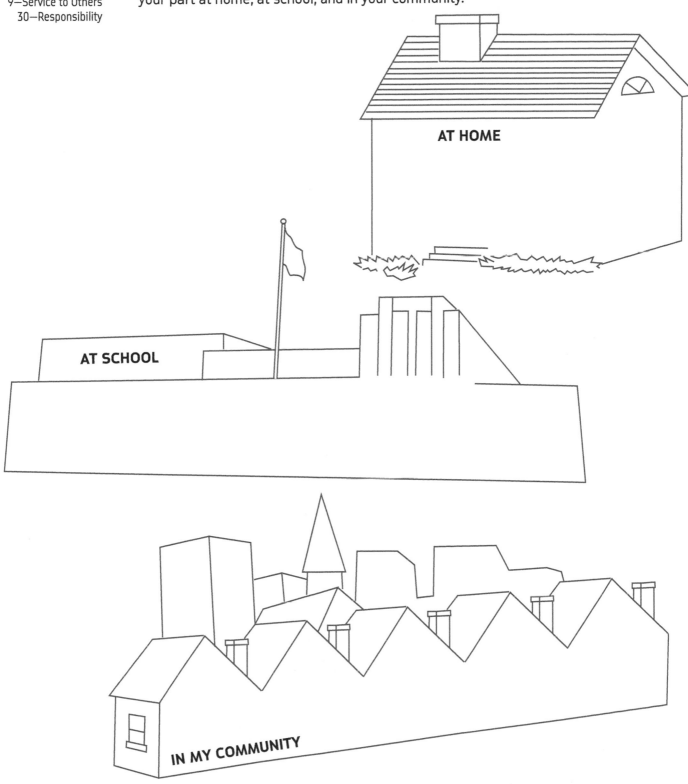

AT HOME

AT SCHOOL

IN MY COMMUNITY

5
Promoting Leadership

All young people are leaders in some way, although they tend to see leaders as people who are in more prominent roles. Adults can help young people develop the leadership skills they need to succeed by encouraging them to tap into their strengths and leadership abilities. Even if young people are quiet and shy, they can learn to set good examples for other people. The activities in this chapter not only build leadership skills, but also help young people see the leadership qualities in themselves and others.

61 | Peacemakers around Us

Focus: Youth create a mural of peacemakers and research qualities of peacemakers.

Developmental Assets Tie-in:

28—Integrity
36—Peaceful Conflict Resolution

You will need:

• a large piece of newsprint or other paper

• a dictionary or access to the Internet

• markers or crayons

• access to a photocopy machine

Activity: Begin the activity by asking young people what a peacemaker is. After some answers are given, encourage youth to look up the term in a dictionary. Discuss why some people are considered peacemakers in a world that continues to experience violence.

On a large piece of paper, have youth draw pictures, hang up photocopies of peacemakers pictured in books, or write the names of peacemakers they know in their communities, their countries, and the world—both living and dead. (Examples of peacemakers include Nelson Mandela, Shirin Ebadi, Elie Wiesel, Wangari Maathai, Mikhail Gorbachev, Jody Williams, the Dalai Lama, Bishop Desmond Tutu, Aung SanSuu Kyi, and Albert Schweitzer. Consult the latest edition of *The World Almanac* or the Internet for a list of Nobel Peace Prize winners if you would like to find more or study people youth may not know much about.)

Form groups of three or four. Have each group choose one peacemaker to research. (You may know of a local peacemaker through your community or your congregation. If so, call the person to ask if he or she would be willing to visit your group—or be interviewed by the group.) Once the smaller groups finish their research, have them report their findings to the whole group.

Discussion Questions:

• *Why are peacemakers important to our community and to the world?*

• *How do people in conflict with peacemakers tend to react to peacemakers? How do peacemakers usually respond? Can you think of specific examples?*

• *What's difficult about being a peacemaker? Why?*

• *What can we do to support peacemakers?*

• *How can you be more of a peacemaker?*

62 | The Meaning of Mentoring

Focus: Youth find out how they can be resources for a mentoring program.

Developmental Assets Tie-in:

8—Youth as Resources

You will need:

• writing paper

• pens or pencils

Note:

This activity will take more than one session. The first session will involve only the youth's participation; the second session will involve the participation of an outside speaker.

Activity: Tell youth that you're inviting a person from a mentoring organization to talk about how and why the organization matches youth and adults with children. Have each youth write down one question they would like to ask the guest. Examples of questions include: What kinds of things do mentors and mentees do together? Who can be a mentor? Who can get a mentor? Why is it important for young people to have mentors?

Collect all the questions and have two or three youth take turns reading them aloud. As a group, agree on five questions that five of the youth will ask the guest from the mentoring organization. Explain that there will be a designated question-and-answer period and if there is time afterward, youth can ask other questions.

Contact a mentoring program, such as One-to-One or Big Brothers Big Sisters, and

ask if someone will speak to your group. If you have funding, you can request a specific topic or speaker. If you do not have funding, ask for a volunteer. Explain that you hope the speaker will invite young people to get involved with the organization.

Have the speaker explain the importance of pairing youth with children and share some of the results of those relationships. Let youth ask their questions, starting with the five that the group agreed upon. After the guest speaker has left, have the group write and send a joint thank-you letter.

Bonus Idea: Encourage youth to consider becoming mentors for younger children or to seek adult mentors for themselves through the organization.

63 | Important Roles

Developmental Assets Tie-in:

8—Youth as Resources
37—Personal Power

Everybody has a number of roles they play in their life. For example, one person can be a daughter, student, sibling, and team leader. Write one important thing you do in each of the designated roles below. For example, in your role as a student you might write that you learn and ask questions; as a family member you participate in family decisions and mow the lawn.

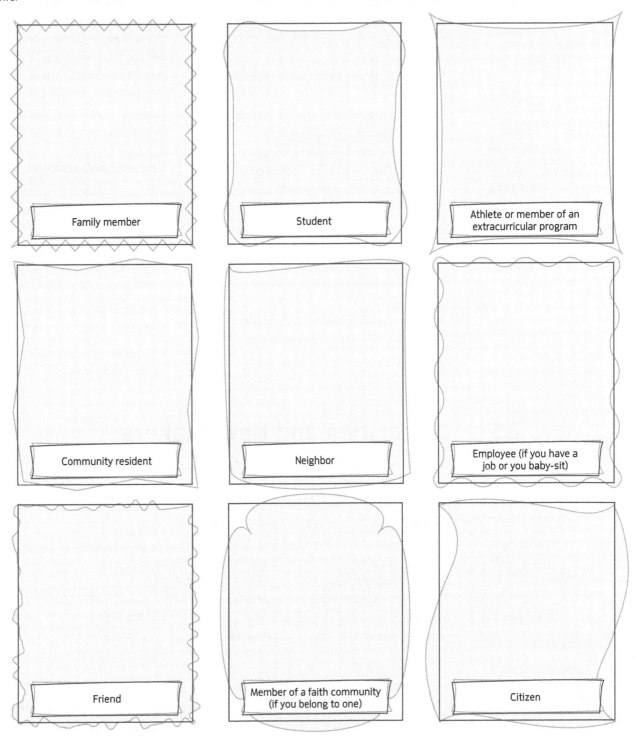

Family member

Student

Athlete or member of an extracurricular program

Community resident

Neighbor

Employee (if you have a job or you baby-sit)

Friend

Member of a faith community (if you belong to one)

Citizen

64 | Classroom Census

Focus: Youth explore the type of support they need because of who they are (depending on whether they are extroverts or introverts).

Developmental Assets Tie-in:

1—Family Support
3—Other Adult Relationships
37—Personal Power
38—Self-Esteem

You will need:

• 10 yellow index cards for each youth

• 10 blue index cards for each youth

Activity: Give each youth 10 yellow index cards and 10 blue ones. Tell youth to place one yellow card in front of them if their answer to the question is "yes" and a blue piece if their answer is "no." Ask youth the following questions one at a time.

1. Overall, do you like to be in the middle of the action?
2. Do you like a lot of variety in your life?
3. Do you know a lot of people?
4. Do you enjoy talking or chitchatting—even with people you don't know well?
5. Are you usually pumped after doing an activity?
6. After you do an activity, are you usually ready to do more right away?
7. Do you tend to talk or act before you think?
8. Overall, do you feel like you have a lot of energy?
9. Do you tend to talk more than listen?
10. Do you like a fast-paced lifestyle?

When everyone has finished, collect the cards that youth did not use. Have each youth count the number of yellow cards and the number of blue cards in front of them, then explain that yellow cards represent extroversion and blue cards represent introversion. Try to stress that one isn't better than the other—extroversion and introversion have to do with a person's response to stimulation and her or his approach to learning.

Discussion Questions:

• *Are most people in this room extroverted (with yellow cards) or introverted (with blue cards)? Explain that more people tend to be extroverted than introverted, but both personality types are equally good. Extroverts like lots of action and people around. Introverts prefer more alone time and doing quiet activities.*

• *Is it important to know whether you're extroverted or introverted? Why or why not?*

• *How does knowing whether you're an extrovert or an introvert affect how you feel about yourself?*

65 | Celebrities and Newsmakers

Focus: Youth identify positive and negative celebrity and "newsmaker" role models.

Developmental Assets Tie-in:

3—Other Adult Relationships
14—Adult Role Models

You will need:

• two sheets of newsprint

• a selection of current teen magazines, sport magazines, and newsmagazines

• scissors

• tape or glue

Activity: Hang two pieces of newsprint on opposite walls. Write "Positive Role Models" at the top of one newsprint and "Negative Role Models" at the top of the other. Distribute recent magazines that youth can cut up.

Ask youth to cut out pictures of celebrities and newsmakers and then tape or glue each picture onto the newsprint sheet they feel is appropriate.

Discussion Questions:

• *Who did you choose for each category? Describe some reasons these people are positive or negative role models.*

• *How easy or difficult was this activity? Why?*

• *Do you think some of the people could appear on both newsprint sheets? Why or why not?*

• *Why are celebrities and newsmakers important?*

• *What are the dangers of idolizing celebrities?*

• *How should we judge whether a celebrity or newsmaker is a worthwhile role model?*

| # Portrait of a Role Model

Developmental Assets Tie-in:

14—Adult Role Models

Which adults do you admire? Choose one of these adults and write her or his name on the line below. Take a moment to think of your role model's qualities and why you look up to him or her, and then write your answers to the questions in the box. What have you learned from watching your role model? Which of the qualities you wrote in the box do you feel *you* have?

ROLE MODEL

MY ROLE MODEL IS

_____

Role-model qualities that I see in myself:

What great things do I say? What words do I use often?

How do I view the world?

How do I treat other people?

What worthwhile things do I do?

How do I put my beliefs into action?

67 | Success at Work

Focus: Youth interview a community leader about her or his assets.

**Developmental
Assets Tie-in:**

14—Adult Role Models
37—Personal Power
39—Sense of Purpose

Activity: As a group, brainstorm leaders in your community whom youth think are successful. Have youth contact two or three of these leaders to see who would be open to a 20-minute conversation with the group. If you have access to transportation, consider doing this activity at the work or volunteer site of these leaders.

Before you meet with the community leader, have youth choose 10 questions they would like to ask the person about his or her assets. Contact the community leader beforehand to ask if he or she would rather receive the questions in advance or answer the questions on the spot.

Some examples of questions could include:

- What was your family life like when you were growing up?
- How important do you think school is for young people?
- What three things were key in helping you become successful?

- What values are important to you? Why?
- What are your strongest skills? Which ones are most challenging for you? Why?
- How much do you have to continue to work at being successful now that you've achieved it?

Discussion Questions:

- *What major points did this leader make when talking about her or his own assets?*
- *What surprised you most about what this leader said?*
- *How are this leader's experiences with assets similar to and different from your own experiences with assets?*
- *What can we learn from this leader about nurturing important assets in our own lives?*

Bonus Idea: Leaders could complete an asset checklist for a peek into their youthful life.

68 | Activity Proposal

Focus: Youth develop an idea for a new activity that gives them a meaningful way to contribute.

**Developmental
Assets Tie-in:**

8—Youth as Resources
9—Service to Others

You will need:

- writing paper
- pens or pencils

Activity: Have youth work together to develop a proposal for an activity they would like to see available in their school, community, congregation, or other organization. Youth may wish to develop a new activity or propose an idea to make an existing activity more meaningful.

Encourage youth to think through details, such as the benefits of the activity, number of youth involved, sponsors, funds needed, and so on. As youth develop the proposal, talk about what they hope to accomplish with the activity and how it will help them grow up healthy and successful.

Once the proposal is fleshed out, have the youth present the proposal to the decision-making body of the organization (such as the principal or student council at a school, the youth group leader or leadership council of a faith community, or the education committee of a community organization).

The proposal might generate positive media attention in your community. Consider asking youth to write letters to a school or local newspaper, explaining their idea (or how they implemented it).

My Idea: *"One of our groups worked to get restaurants to go smoke-free, and it worked. We use this idea in our weekly Youth in Action projects."*
—James Robinson, Bowling Green, Kentucky

If you were to read the resume of a good leader, what would it say? In the spaces below, write your answers:

Developmental Assets Tie-in:

14—Adult Role Models
16—High Expectations
21—Achievement Motivation

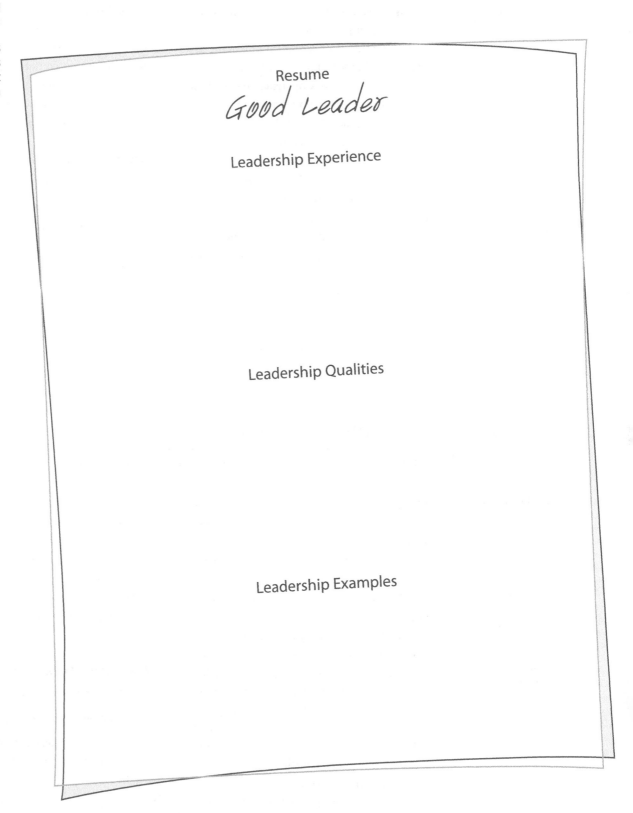

Resume

Good Leader

Leadership Experience

Leadership Qualities

Leadership Examples

| # The Leaders Around You

Focus: Youth analyze the qualities of leaders they know.

Developmental Assets Tie-in:

The Developmental Assets Framework

You will need:

• eight pieces of newsprint

• masking or painter's tape

• a lot of small sticky notes (or Post-it Notes)

• markers

• a pen for each young person

• a photocopy of the Developmental Assets among Youth list on page 18 for each young person

Activity: Have young people form groups of eight. Give each group one piece of newsprint. Tell each group that they represent one of the asset categories: Support, Empowerment, Boundaries and Expectations, Constructive Use of Time, Commitment to Learning, Positive Values, Social Competencies, and Positive Identity. Distribute photocopies of the Developmental Assets list from page 18 for each young person.

Have each group write their asset category at the top of their newsprint and then hang it somewhere in the room.

Give each young person a pen and some small sticky notes. Ask the group to think about the individuals they know (both young people and adults) who are leaders in your organization, school, or community.

Ask young people to write a quality of one leader on a sticky note that fits the asset category represented by their group. For example,

under "Support," a leader might have strong support from family members and may also support others. Give young people about one minute to write something different on each sticky note and attach it to the newsprint. Then have them switch to another newsprint and repeat the activity. Do this a total of eight times.

Discussion Questions:

• *What did you discover about our leaders?*

• *How does the Developmental Assets framework highlight qualities of leaders?*

• *How could the Developmental Assets framework build your leadership skills?*

| # The Leader in You

Focus: Youth name different leadership qualities they have.

Developmental Assets Tie-in:

The Developmental Assets Framework

You will need:

• a one-pound bag of M&M candies

• a photocopy of the Developmental Assets among Youth list on page 18 for each young person

Activity: Have young people sit in a circle. Give each young person a photocopy of the Developmental Assets list from page 18. Pass around the bag of M&M candies and say that each person can take anywhere from 3 to 10 pieces. Sit with the group and take 10 pieces of candy for yourself.

Say that this activity is about leadership skills. Explain that everyone is going to take turns naming their leadership qualities (they can use the list of Developmental Assets for ideas), and they need to name the number of qualities according to the number of pieces of candy they took. Once they have named the correct number of qualities, they can eat their candy while the person next to them starts.

Most likely young people will groan, but you also can groan because you took 10 pieces

of candy. Start with yourself to model how the activity works and say things like "I am responsible because I pay my bills on time" and "I am a positive example to others." Continue the activity until everyone in the group has had a turn. If anyone struggles for ideas, encourage others in the group to name a leadership quality in that person.

Discussion Questions:

• *What did you discover during this activity?*

• *Can anyone be a leader? Why or why not?*

• *Why is it hard to name our own leadership qualities? Why is it easier to see the leadership qualities of others?*

• *Why is it important to recognize the leadership qualities in ourselves?*

| # Asset Builder Check-Up

Developmental Assets Tie-in:

The Developmental Assets Framework

It's exciting to dream about the future and make plans for the great things you will do. As you consider your future, think about the other people who will be there—as neighbors, co-workers, friends, and residents in the same community. Your skills as an asset builder with children and younger youth today will affect the quality of your community today and tomorrow! Grade yourself on these asset-building actions. Consider how to incorporate more asset building for children and younger youth into your plans for each day.

	I do this often	I do this once in a while	I have never done this
I smile and say "hi" to children and younger youth when I see them.	❑	❑	❑
I am a role model of caring language and positive actions for children and younger youth.	❑	❑	❑
I attend games or concerts of young people I know and cheer for them.	❑	❑	❑
I watch for children while driving or riding my bike because I know they often run out into the street.	❑	❑	❑
I encourage younger people to join in when I'm helping others.	❑	❑	❑
I help children and younger youth learn or practice new skills.	❑	❑	❑
I sing or read to young children.	❑	❑	❑
I ask younger people to be caring and responsible.	❑	❑	❑
I appreciate the talents and abilities that children and younger youth have—and I tell them so.	❑	❑	❑

6
Strengthening Relationships

To grow up healthy, young people need support, love, and encouragement from caring, principled adults. They need homes, schools, organizations, and communities that are accepting, affirming, and safe. This chapter presents activities for helping youth understand the importance of developing strong relationships.

73 | The Family History of Talk

Focus: Youth talk with their parents about their parents' teenage experiences.

Developmental Assets Tie-in:

1—Family Support
2—Positive Family Communication

Activity: Have youth talk to their parents about their parents' growing-up years. Encourage the young people to ask a lot of questions to find out how their parents' family dynamics were both similar to and different from their own family dynamics. They might ask questions such as:

- What did you think of your parents when you were a teenager?
- What are some of your best memories of your parents when you were a teenager?
- What kinds of things did you most often talk about in your family?
- Which topics were hard to talk about with your parents? Why?
- Who did most of the disciplining?
- Who did most of the household chores?
- What did you think about your parents' job(s)?
- What did you like best about your family? Why?

- What did you like least? Why?
- Which rituals or traditions (such as always eating one meal together a day) did your family have that you really liked? Why?
- What do you think of the way your parents raised you now that you're a parent yourself?

Have youth report what they learned to the group. Talk about similarities and differences.

Discussion Questions:

- *What was it like to ask your parents these kinds of questions?*
- *Which questions got the longest answers? The shortest?*
- *What surprised you the most?*
- *How similar to or different from your own lives were your parents' childhood and teenage years?*
- *What can you learn from this experience about how to communicate with and relate to your parents?*

74 | Passionate People

Focus: Youth interview people who find meaning through their interests and passions.

Developmental Assets Tie-in:

14—Adult Role Models
39—Sense of Purpose

Activity: Have each young person identify an adult in his or her extended family, neighborhood, school, or other organization to interview. Explain that the purpose of the interview is to find out what gives the person meaning in life.

Before the young people do the interviews, brainstorm a list of four or five questions that will help them find out what makes the person really tick. Some sample questions might include: What do you really enjoy doing? What activities are you really passionate about? If you could choose one thing to do with your time, and did not need to worry about money or other responsibilities, what would you do? What gives you meaning in life? Why?

Have youth conduct their interviews and then share what they found out with the rest of the group.

Discussion Questions:

- *Was it easy for this person to articulate how he or she finds meaning in life? Why or why not?*
- *Do you think most people know what gives them purpose? Why or why not?*
- *What gives you purpose?*
- *If you're not sure what gives you purpose, how can you find out?*
- *Do you think it's important for people to have a sense of purpose? Why or why not?*

You are often busy. Your parent(s) are often busy. Your teachers are often busy. But it is important for schools and families to connect in order to build assets—despite their hectic schedules.

Think about your family's schedule. Then check the ways that you think your parent(s) could be involved in your school.

After you finish filling out the "According to Youth" column, show the worksheet to your parent(s) or guardian(s) and ask her or him to complete the "According to Parent" column. When the whole worksheet is filled out, compare your answers with the answers your parent(s) gave. Talk with your parent(s) about ways to increase their involvement in your schooling.

Developmental Assets Tie-in:

1—Family Support
6—Parent Involvement in Schooling

Good Ways for Your Parent(s) to Get Involved in School:	According to Youth	According to Parent
1. Ask young person what happened in school each day.	☐	☐
2. Set aside time for young person to do homework each day.	☐	☐
3. Create a space for young person to do homework at home.	☐	☐
4. Help youth with homework.	☐	☐
5. Periodically call a teacher to check on young person's progress.	☐	☐
6. Participate in a parent-teacher organization.	☐	☐
7. Attend a school board meeting to learn what some of the key issues are.	☐	☐
8. Go to parent-teacher conferences.	☐	☐
9. Send a teacher a note of encouragement.	☐	☐
10. Volunteer to help out at the school.	☐	☐
11. Other _____.	☐	☐

76 | Who Supports You?

Focus: Youth think of all the different adults they can go to for support.

Developmental Assets Tie-in:

1—Family Support
3—Other Adult Relationships
4—Caring Neighborhood
5—Caring School Climate

You will need:

- chalkboard and chalk (or newsprint and a marker)

Activity: Have youth brainstorm types of adults (other than parents) who are good at providing advice and support. Encourage youth to think of the adults they usually go to as well as other adults they have never gone to, but could. For example, a young person might name a neighbor, a mentor, a boss, a coach, an uncle, a religious youth worker, a teacher, an older sister, and so on. Record all their ideas on newsprint or a chalkboard. Don't discard or evaluate any of their ideas.

When you finish the list, note how many different types of adults can provide support. Then create another list of qualities that make these people good sources of advice and support. For example, youth might list qualities such as patience, understanding, good eye contact, sense of humor, and good listening skills.

Discussion Questions:

- *What difference does it make to have an adult like this in your life?*
- *How would you tell a friend to go about finding a caring adult friend if he or she didn't have one to turn to?*
- *Name one adult, other than your parents, whom you would like to get to know better. Why did you choose that person?*
- *How can you go out of your way to see that person this week?*

77 | Unclear Boundaries

Focus: Youth experience what happens when rules aren't articulated well.

Developmental Assets Tie-in:

11—Family Boundaries
12—School Boundaries
13—Neighborhood Boundaries

You will need:

- 150 toothpicks
- 150 gumdrops
- chalkboard and chalk (or newsprint and markers)

Activity: Form three equal groups of players. Make lots of room since the teams will be working independently and should not be able to see what the other teams are doing. Hand out 50 toothpicks and 50 gumdrops to each group. To one group, whisper (so that the other groups cannot hear) that they can eat as many gumdrops as they wish in the course of building their structure, but must do so discreetly so the other groups don't notice that they aren't using all the gumdrops. Explain that they can stick as many toothpicks as they wish into each gumdrop in order to use all 50 toothpicks.

Stand at the front of the room and instruct the whole group to build a structure using the toothpicks and the gumdrops. Tell them the goal is to be the first group to finish, but that they must use all of their toothpicks and gumdrops.

Then have the groups begin. Once a group wins, stop the activity. Have the groups examine the winning structure.

Discussion Questions:

- *How do you feel about the structure the winning team made? Why?*
- *Did the winning team follow the rules given? Why or why not?*
- *Was the game set up fairly?*
- *What would have happened if every group had been given the same instructions?*
- *What experiences have you had when rules weren't articulated well or were confusing?*
- *Why do you think rules aren't always clear?*

| # The Valuable You

**Developmental
Assets Tie-in:**

1—Family Support
3—Other Adult
Relationships
7—Community
Values Youth

We don't always realize that we're valued by other people. Identify four adults, including your parent(s), an adult relative, and one or two other adults in your life, such as a teacher, coach, boss, youth group leader, or neighbor. In the "ribbon" on each of the diamonds below, write the name of one of those people.

Call or visit each of these four people and ask them why they think you're a valuable person. For example, you could call and say something like, "Hi, I'm calling as part of a project for my youth group. I am supposed to interview four adults in my life, and I picked you as one of my favorites. Can you tell me why you think I'm a valuable person?"

People always know, and what they say may surprise you. After you talk with all four adults, write what each person said in the box under the diamond labeled with their name.

| **Disaster Control**

Focus: Youth decide how best to cope with a difficult situation.

Developmental Assets Tie-in:

37—Personal Power
40—Positive View of Personal Future

Activity: Have youth form groups of three or four. Explain that each group should imagine they live near a river and heavy rains have suddenly come, flooding the area. Each group must work together to choose only three items that would help them get through the situation. They can choose any three items they would like.

Give the groups 10–15 minutes to hash things out before they report their three items to the larger group.

Discussion Questions:

- *How did having the opportunity to choose any three items help you in this difficult situation? Why?*

- *How would you have felt if I told you that you could do nothing and just needed to let the flood damage your homes and community?*

- *When bad things happen, do you usually feel you have some choice and power to deal with the situation? Why or why not?*

- *How do bad events affect how you feel about the future?*

- *Is it important to have personal power? Why or why not?*

---

80 | **Back-to-Back Answers**

Focus: Youth practice answering questions about their school experience.

Developmental Assets Tie-in:

1—Family Support
2—Positive Family Communication

You will need:

- masking tape
- pencils or pens
- writing paper

Activity: Cut sheets of writing paper into fourths and give each youth one piece. Ask youth to close their eyes and think about what happens at the end of a typical school day, answering these questions silently:

- Where do you go after school?
- Who are you with after school?
- What do you usually do after school?
- At what time do you first see your parent or some other caring adult in your household?
- What questions about school do you usually hear from your parent or other caring adult?
- Do parents ask the right questions? Are there questions they could ask to show how much they care?

Ask youth to open their eyes and write one question about their school day that they commonly hear from parents or guardians on a slip of paper, folding it so no one else can see it. Gather the slips of paper and mix them up. Then tape one to the back of each youth without telling her or him what it says. Ask youth to form pairs and then instruct one person to be the "youth" and the other to be the "parent." The "youth" should look at the question on the "parent's" back, read it silently, then answer it out loud. The "parent" gets two tries to guess what the question is. Partners then switch roles.

Discussion Questions:

- *What information about school is important to share with your parents?*

- *Do you ever feel like you don't want to tell your parents about school? Why or why not?*

- *What could your parents do to improve their communication with you about school? What could you do?*

Developmental Assets Tie-in:

2—Positive Family Communication
33—Interpersonal Competence

People tend to be good at some relationship skills and not as good at others. Below are questions that will help you rate yourself on several aspects that are important in developing a relationship. (Be honest!) The scale is from 1 to 5, with 1 being the lowest (skills you really need to work on) and 5 being the highest (skills you have already developed very well). At the end of the list, add some other relationship skills that you think are important.

After you finish, circle one of the skills to which you gave a low rating but would like to work on. For the next week, make a deliberate effort to improve this relationship-building skill.

SKILLS	RATING				
	Needs work				Well developed
Starting conversations with someone you don't know very well.	1	2	3	4	5
Calling someone on a regular basis.	1	2	3	4	5
Asking someone her or his opinion on an issue.	1	2	3	4	5
Telling someone when he or she hurts your feelings.	1	2	3	4	5
Doing something you have in common with someone.	1	2	3	4	5
Listening to a person when he or she needs to talk.	1	2	3	4	5
Telling someone how you really feel about her or him.	1	2	3	4	5
Complimenting someone for something he or she did that you liked.	1	2	3	4	5
Doing something nice for someone because you feel like it.	1	2	3	4	5
Hanging out with someone because you like the person.	1	2	3	4	5
_____	1	2	3	4	5
_____	1	2	3	4	5

Focus: Youth honor the contributions that adults have made to their lives.

Developmental Assets Tie-in:

3—Other Adult Relationships
4—Caring Neighborhood
5—Caring School Climate

You will need:

• a camera (or ask each youth to bring a photo of an adult, other than a parent or guardian, who is important to her or him)

• construction paper

• markers

• newsprint

• scissors

• staplers

• tape

Note:

This activity may take more than one session.

Activity: Hang the piece of newsprint where the whole group can see it. Invite youth to think of adults—other than their parents—who are important to them. Have the group discuss how these adults have shown support to them while you record their answers on the newsprint.

Now have each young person identify one such adult in her or his own life and imagine an award that could be given to this person (such as Best E-mailer, Most Positive Outlook, Giver of Great Advice about Cars, Most Fun to Play Cards With, Friendliest Face in School, or Most Encouraging). If there are youth who cannot identify any adults for this exercise, ask them to think of the kind of support they wish they could have, make an award for that, and attach it to a drawing of an adult labeled "Could you support a young person in this way?" (To take this a step further, you might try to connect these young people with an adult through a local mentoring organization. Also, you could ask some other caring adults to volunteer their time with one of the young people.)

Create a bulletin board display that honors these important adults. Ask youth to take photos of the adults they admire or use photos they've brought with them. Post the photos and make "award medals" from construction paper to announce the award and tell one example of what this person did to earn it. Ask a few youth to cut large letters to spell out "Honor Roll."

Discussion Questions:

• Would any of these adults be surprised to find their picture on this bulletin board? Why?

• How do you let these adults know that you appreciate the support they give you? Why is this important?

• How do others let you know that the support you give is appreciated?

My Idea: *"Center this project on people at their school. Invite recipients of the awards to see the bulletin board."*
—Nancy Tellett-Royce, Minneapolis, Minnesota

Relationships give meaning to our lives. The caring, positive relationships we have are like gifts. On the gift tag below, write as many things as you can think of that make your life better and more meaningful because of the relationships you have.

Developmental Assets Tie-in:

1—Family Support
3—Other Adult Relationships
4—Caring Neighborhood
15—Positive Peer Influence

84 | Your Neighborhood

Focus: Youth analyze the neighborhood they live in.

Developmental Assets Tie-in:

4—Caring Neighborhood
7—Community Values Youth

You will need:

• paper for each young person

• markers

Activity: Hand out paper and markers and have youth draw a picture of their neighborhood, including the homes of their neighbors, whether they live in a house, an apartment, or a rural area. Encourage them to be creative if they live in the country where their neighbors are miles away or in an apartment building where many of the neighbors they know are right down the hall.

After youth finish drawing the layout of their neighborhood, have them write the names of people and pets who live nearby. If they aren't sure of names, have them describe what they know about the occupants. For example, someone might write that she knows that a man, woman, teenage girl, and black dog live two doors down. If young people aren't sure who lives where, but have a guess about the occupant, have them write that too.

Discussion Questions:

• *How many neighbors do you know well?*

• *What do you think your neighbors know about you?*

• *How do you feel about your neighbors?*

• *Which neighbors seem friendly? Scary?*

• *Why is it important to know your neighbors?*

My Idea: *"We do this in small groups with art supplies to create a developmentally attentive community and then have small groups share what they've created."*

—Flora Sanchez, Albuquerque, New Mexico

85 | Close Friends and Family

Focus: Youth identify moments in their lives when they felt close to someone.

Developmental Assets Tie-in:

1—Family Support
3—Other Adult Relationships
4—Caring Neighborhood
15—Positive Peer Influence

Activity: Ask young people to think of two moments in their lives when they have felt very close to someone (perhaps a family member, friend, neighbor, teacher, or someone else).

Have them take turns describing these experiences to the group, and encourage them to explain why these moments stick out in their minds. If you wish, invite group members to ask questions after each person has spoken.

Discussion Questions:

• *What makes you feel close to someone? Why?*

• *Why is it important to be close to other people?*

• *What do you do when relationships change? What happens when a close relationship becomes distant or strained?*

• *What can you do in your current relationships to make them stronger?*

Developmental Assets Tie-in:

1—Family Support
3—Other Adult Relationships
4—Caring Neighborhood
5—Caring School Climate
14—Adult Role Models

Whom do you trust? To whom would you go if you needed advice? Who can keep your secrets? In the spaces below, write the names of five adults you trust. Consider family members (including aunts, uncles, and grandparents), teachers, coaches, neighbors, adult friends of your family, employers, adults in your faith community, club leaders, counselors, and more. Keep this list so that the next time you need an adult to turn to, you will know where to go.

1. _____

2. _____

3. _____

4. _____

5. _____

Focus: Youth experiment with peer influence and its effect on decision making.

Activity: Write each of the following instructions on a separate index card. Each youth will need one card, so repeat some of them if necessary.

- Convince a person on your team to pop a balloon.
- Convince a person on another team to give you that team's tape.
- Convince a person on your team to work faster.
- Convince a person on your team to quit.
- Convince your team to use materials in addition to the ones provided.
- Convince a person on your team to rip a newspaper into shreds.
- Convince a person on your team to cheer on your team.
- Convince a person on your team to "trash talk" another team.

Distribute index cards to the group, then instruct everyone to read the card silently before hiding it in their pocket or somewhere else so others cannot read it. Tell youth that during the game they should follow the instructions on the card and keep mental notes of how successful or unsuccessful they are in carrying out the instructions. Suggest that they be subtle about what their "role" is so that others won't catch on too quickly.

After you have explained the purpose of the cards, have youth form teams of four. Tell each team that its challenge is to build a structure at least 12 inches tall that will support two inflated balloons. The teams will have five minutes to complete the structure, and the first team to finish is the winner. Give each team a stack of old newspapers, a roll of masking tape, and two inflated balloons. Give a start signal and stand back.

Call time after five minutes and applaud the winners. Gather as a group and ask each young person to report on the task from her or his index card.

Discussion Questions:

- *How well did your team work together? Why?*
- *Were you able to do what was instructed on the index card? What did you do to try to persuade another person? Was this easy or challenging for you? Why?*
- *How do friends influence each other?*
- *Did you feel pressure to do what the others in your group were suggesting?*
- *What factors influenced your decision about whether or not to be persuaded?*

My Friendship Circles

Developmental Assets Tie-in:

15—Positive Peer Influence
33—Interpersonal Competence

Not all friends are the same. You may have some very close friends. You probably have some social friends, and others you do things with once in a while. As you think about classmates or other youth in your community, some of them are probably just acquaintances—other youth you know, but who aren't part of your social life. Answer the questions below to consider how each of these groups is an important part of your life.

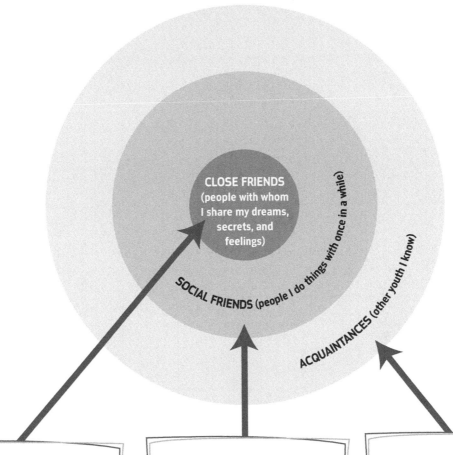

CLOSE FRIENDS (people with whom I share my dreams, secrets, and feelings)

SOCIAL FRIENDS (people I do things with once in a while)

ACQUAINTANCES (other youth I know)

What does this group of my friends have in common with the other groups?	What does this group of my friends have in common with the other groups?	What does this group of my friends have in common with the other groups?
How is this group of my friends different?	How is this group of my friends different?	How is this group of my friends different?
Benefits I get from having this group of friends:	Benefits I get from having this group of friends:	Benefits I get from having this group of friends:
What I contribute to this group of friends:	What I contribute to this group of friends:	What I contribute to this group of friends:

7
Improving Communication

When young people have good communication

skills they are better equipped for success.

They need to know how to express their needs,

desires, and opinions, and they also need to know

how to negotiate with others in times of hope

and conflict. The activities in this chapter present

creative ways for young people to successfully

communicate with members of their families,

their friends, and other adults in their lives.

89 | School Census

Focus: Youth conduct a survey on school climate.

Developmental Assets Tie-in:

5—Caring School Climate
22—School Engagement
24—Bonding to School

You will need:

• a copy machine

• paper

Note:

This activity may take more than one session.

Activity: Have youth get approval to conduct a survey of students in their school about school climate. Depending on how many youth are present, create small groups and ask each one to create a list of questions that, together, would equal 20 questions. (For example, if you have four groups, have each group come up with 5 questions.) After groups finish, have each group report on their list. Then have youth agree on 20 multiple-choice questions to include.

Encourage the young people to think of questions that measure students' opinions about school climate. For example, they may ask:

• How caring and encouraging do you think our school is?

  ❑ Very caring ❑ Somewhat caring
  ❑ Not caring at all

• What do you like best about our school?

  ❑ Open lunches ❑ State basketball champions
  ❑ Most youth graduate ❑ Study hall
  ❑ Other _____

• What do you like least about our school?

  ❑ Too many suspensions
  ❑ Graffiti on the walls
  ❑ Poor selection in vending machines
  ❑ Not enough class choices
  ❑ Other _____

• Who tends to show a lot of care toward students? (Check all that apply.)

  ❑ Teachers ❑ Coaches ❑ Administrators
  ❑ Aides ❑ Extracurricular adult leaders
  ❑ Other students ❑ Custodians
  ❑ Other _____

After choosing 20 questions, have the group create and duplicate the survey. Distribute surveys and decide on a plan to collect and tabulate them. Ask for volunteers to copy results from each survey onto one master copy. Then ask one or two youth to calculate totals and percentages for each question.

Talk about how to distribute the findings.

Bonus Idea: If you're not located in a school, have youth survey the climate of your program or organization.

90 | Perceptions of Community Perceptions

Focus: Youth monitor others in the community to judge community perceptions of young people.

Developmental Assets Tie-in:

7—Community Values Youth
32—Planning and Decision Making

You will need:

• writing paper

• pens or pencils

Activity: Have youth form teams of four (more or less). Have each team create a list of ways to judge public perceptions of youth. Ideas could include adults making eye contact with youth, adults greeting youth, adults smiling at youth, and so on. Encourage young people to make a list of five to six items that would be easily measurable.

Then, have each team do a 10-minute monitoring of an area where there are a lot of adults, such as a shopping mall, a fellowship area before a religious service, a community event or game, a busy sidewalk, or other high-traffic spot.

Discussion Questions:

• *Overall, how would you say most of the adults in your study perceived the youth in your group? Why?*

• *What are some of the ways the adults interacted with youth?*

• *What would happen if you repeated the activity but also made more of an effort to smile, make eye contact, and greet the adults? Why?*

• *How do you think that could change? Who has the power to start that change?*

My Idea: *"Share the results with adult groups."*
—Pamela Brock, Elkhart, Indiana

Developmental Assets Tie-in:

1—Family Support
2—Positive Family Communication

Communication with your family is essential, but it's not always easy. Even in the most caring families, certain topics are avoided. All families experience time pressures that make it a challenge to sit down and talk together. Which topics do you wish you had more time to talk about with your parent(s) or guardian(s) or other caring adults at home? Fold this paper in half vertically. Write the topics you'd like to discuss near one phone. Ask a parent or guardian to fill in topics in the box near the other phone. Compare your lists. How can you begin one of these conversations?

SCHOOL TRIP

CHOICES OF CLOTHING   COLLEGE   PARTIES   USING THE CAR   PHONE TIME

SUMMER JOB   FRIENDS   CHORES   DRUGS   MOVIES

EXPECTATIONS   SCHOOL ACTIVITIES

INTERNET USE   MONEY   NEEDS OF OLDER RELATIVES   SEX   GRADES   SIBLINGS

CLEANING MY ROOM   FAVORS   DATING   VACATION   FAMILY PROBLEMS   CURFEWS

Focus: Youth compare parents' standards on a variety of issues.

Developmental Assets Tie-in:

11—Family Boundaries
30—Responsibility

You will need:

- four empty one-pound cans (such as coffee cans)

- several sheets of white paper

- scissors

- access to a copy machine

Activity: Bring the cans to the group. On a piece of paper write these items (or any others that are appropriate for your group): clothing, weekend curfew, weekday curfew, use of the car, dating, part-time work, extracurricular activities, friends, homework, asking for something, mealtime etiquette, expressing anger, expressing sadness, celebrating, drinking alcohol, and TV viewing.

Make three photocopies of this paper; then cut each piece of paper into strips so that each strip has only one item written on it. Put all the strips from one paper into one can, and do the same with the other papers and cans.

Have youth form four teams; then, give each team a can. Have youth take turns taking out one piece of paper at a time and reading it aloud. Ask each person to share with the team what boundaries her or his parents have for that item. (If parents haven't set boundaries on that topic, youth may say what they think their parents

would want them to do.) Each youth should keep her or his strip of paper and pass the can to the person on her or his left, who will then follow the steps of the activity. Have everyone continue taking turns until all the strips of paper are drawn.

Discussion Questions:

- *What common boundaries do parents set for youth?*

- *Do most parents set reasonable boundaries? Too strict? Too lenient? Why do you think that is?*

- *How do your parents decide on the boundaries they establish for you (for example, based on personal experience, a conversation you have as a family, what they think is "right," their religious beliefs)?*

- *How would your life be better or worse if your parents didn't set boundaries?*

- *What would you tell a friend who had major disagreements with a parent about boundaries?*

Focus: Youth affirm each other by writing positive messages.

Developmental Assets Tie-in:

38—Self-Esteem

You will need:

- scissors

- one sheet of red construction paper for each youth

- one safety pin for each youth

- a pen or pencil for each youth

Activity: Have each youth cut a large heart out of the construction paper; then ask them to help each other pin their hearts to the backs of their shirts.

Ask youth to walk around the room and write something positive on each person's heart. For example, they might write: "I like your smile," "You're a great listener," or "I admire your ability to do well in math."

After the young people finish writing, have them help each other remove the hearts from their shirts. Give everyone time to read the messages on their hearts.

Discussion Questions:

- *What are some of the messages you got today that really give you a boost?*

- *How did it feel to take time to make other people feel good about themselves?*

- *What was it like writing positive messages to others, knowing that people were also writing positive messages on your heart?*

- *How important is it to say nice things to other people? Why?*

- *What are ways young people can enhance their own self-esteem and the self-esteem of their friends?*

If you were the parent, at what age would you allow your child—if ever—to do the following activities?

Developmental Assets Tie-in:

11—Family Boundaries
30—Responsibility

Responsibility	Age	Why That Age?
1. Wear makeup	_____	_____
2. Have a credit card	_____	_____
3. Work part-time during the school year	_____	_____
4. Drink alcohol for the first time	_____	_____
5. Get her or his ears pierced	_____	_____
6. Buy a car	_____	_____
7. Go on a group date	_____	_____
8. Go on an individual date	_____	_____
9. Date someone exclusively	_____	_____
10. Stay out until midnight on weekends	_____	_____
11. Not have a curfew	_____	_____
12. Rent a hotel room	_____	_____
13. Have a boy/girl party	_____	_____
14. Open a checking account	_____	_____
15. Get a tattoo	_____	_____
16. Stay home alone when parents go out of town	_____	_____
17. Take a weekend camping trip with peers	_____	_____
18. Go to an R-rated movie	_____	_____
19. Go out of state with a friend's family	_____	_____
20. Fly unaccompanied on an airplane	_____	_____

95 | Following the Leader

Focus: Youth follow various ways of modeling.

Developmental Assets Tie-in:

3—Other Adult Relationships
14—Adult Role Models

Activity: Form a large circle. Explain that you want youth to follow your verbal instructions, not your actions. Tell everyone to jump up and down while you sit down. Ask them to run in place while you walk slowly from one part of the circle to the other. Have them yawn while you smile and wink at them.

Stop the action. Explain that you now want everyone to follow your actions, not your words. Start spinning around in place while saying, "Don't spin." Then hop on one foot while saying, "No hopping, only sitting is allowed." Then start yelling, "Don't yell anymore. Just whisper! Do you hear me? Whisper! Whisper! Whisper!"

Stop the action. Explain that you want youth to follow your instructions. Have everyone march while you march. Then have them sit down as you sit down. Then have them hold hands in the circle as you hold your neighbor's hand.

Discussion Questions:

- *How did it feel to follow my verbal instructions when I was doing the opposite of what I was asking you to do? Why?*

- *How did it feel to follow my actions when my words contradicted what I was doing? Why?*

- *What do you think of adults who say "Do as I say, not as I do"?*

- *Was it more difficult to follow the verbal instructions with the contradictory actions or the actions with the contradictory words? Why?*

- *Why is it important for role models and leaders to do what they want others to do?*

96 | Following the Safe Path

Focus: Youth observe positive and negative peer pressure.

Developmental Assets Tie-in:

35—Resistance Skills

You will need:

- one blindfold

Activity: Ask for one volunteer who is willing to be blindfolded; then ask that person to leave the room for a few minutes. With the rest of the group, set up a safe maze of obstacles, using chairs, desks, and other objects in the room. Make sure the maze has a fairly wide walkway. Explain that when you come back with the volunteer, that person will be blindfolded and youth are to yell out advice that will cause the volunteer to bump into objects.

Leave the room to tell the volunteer you're going to blindfold him or her. Explain that he or she will be going through an obstacle course blindfolded and will need to listen to you whisper advice on which way to go. Encourage the volunteer to move very slowly because there will be chairs and desks in the way.

Blindfold the volunteer and return to the room together. Start the activity. Stay close to the volunteer, keeping her or him safe while constantly whispering good advice.

Afterward, take the blindfold off the volunteer and bring the group together.

Discussion Questions:

- *As the volunteer, whom did you trust at first? Why? Whom did you learn to trust? Why?*

- *Why did you eventually resist doing what the masses were saying?*

- *How hard was it to listen to me once you realized most people were pressuring you to make wrong turns?*

- *How was this activity similar to real-life peer pressure and dangerous situations? Why?*

- *How can strong resistance skills help you?*

In each of the talk bubbles below, write one expectation—for example, in the "Parents" bubble, you might write, "Mom expects me to do well in school." After you finish, put a star next to those whose expectations and encouragement help you in positive ways.

Developmental Assets Tie-in:

16—High Expectations

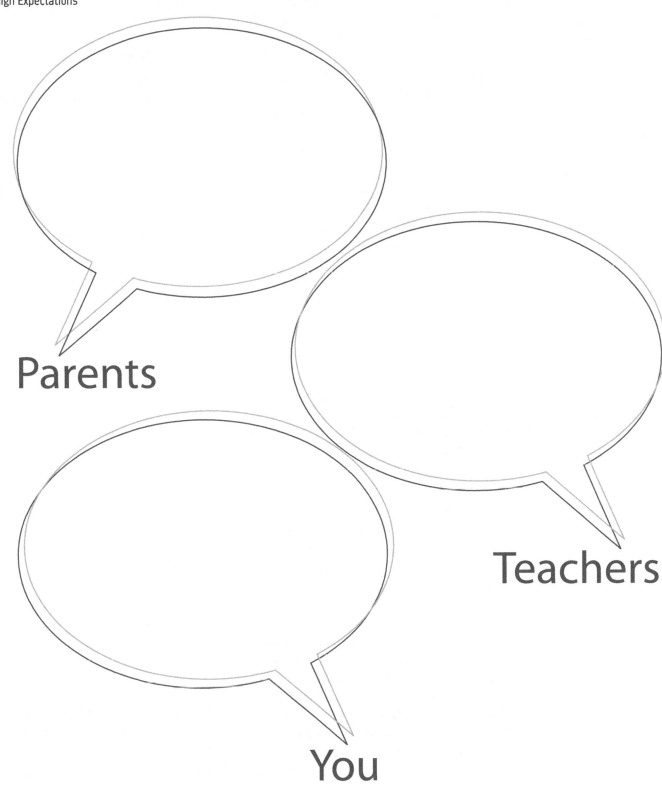

Parents

Teachers

You

| 98 | # Motivating Walk |

Focus: Youth experience and discuss the difference between encouragement and discouragement.

Developmental Assets Tie-in:

21—Achievement Motivation
37—Personal Power

You will need:

• some type of blindfold for each pair of youth

• newsprint and a marker (or chalkboard and chalk)

Activity: Ask each youth to find a partner. Give each pair a piece of cloth or a handkerchief to use as a blindfold and have one person blindfold the other. On newsprint or a chalkboard, write "Keep telling your partner that he or she can't do it as you lead her or him around the room. Don't give any encouragement."

Then say something like "We're now going to have the sighted partners lead the blindfolded partners from one end of the room to the other. Begin now."

Observe what happens. After everyone has moved the length of the room, stop the activity. On the chalkboard or newsprint, write: "This time, give your partner lots of support and encouragement."

Aloud, say something like: "Okay, let's do this activity again. Begin."

After everyone has moved to the other part of the room, stop the activity and have youth remove their blindfolds.

Discussion Questions:

• *Those of you who were blindfolded—what were you thinking as you were being led around the room?*

• *Which time was easier for the blindfolded youth? Why?*

• *How did it feel to get only negative feedback? Only positive?*

• *How did it feel to give only negative feedback? Only positive?*

• *Which is more motivating: negative or positive feedback? Why?*

• *What type of feedback do most young people get about school? What impact does it have?*

• *What are some things that are most motivating to you in school and learning?*

| 99 | # The Benefits of Caring |

Focus: Youth demonstrate how caring and uncaring behavior affects their attitudes about school.

Developmental Assets Tie-in:

5—Caring School Climate
24—Bonding to School
26—Caring
38—Self-Esteem

Activity: Form two groups of youth and separate the groups from each other. Quietly talk with one group so that youth from the other group can't hear. Say that you want each person to choose an affirming comment to make, such as "You're great" or "I like your smile." Encourage them to make it personal, and suggest that each person choose a different comment.

Then quietly talk with the other group so that youth from the first group can't hear you. Say that you want each person to think of a discouraging comment to make, choosing one of the following: "Stop that." "Is that the best you can do?" "I don't like that." (If you add other comments, make sure they aren't hurtful in personal ways.)

Explain to everyone that you want the two groups to break up and mingle around the room. When you say, "Stop," each person should pair up with someone nearby and take turns saying their encouraging or discouraging comment to the other person. Each time you say, "Stop," youth should find new partners and repeat the same messages they chose originally.

Do the activity four or five times.

Discussion Questions:

• *Which people did you enjoy talking with? Why?*

• *Which people did you not enjoy exchanging comments with? Why?*

• *How do the people at your school interact with each other? How does this affect how you feel about your school?*

• *Overall, do you care about your school? Why or why not?*

• *Why are students more apt to care about their schools when they're in positive, encouraging environments?*

100 | School Wish List

In each of the areas below, write two ideas that would help make your school a national model of a caring, encouraging school environment.

Developmental Assets Tie-in:

5—Caring School Climate
22—School Engagement
24—Bonding to School

Relationships among students

1.

2.

Extracurricular activities

1.

2.

Student-teacher relationships

1.

2.

Administration

1.

2.

School environment/building

1.

2.

Student government/student council

1.

2.

School social functions

1.

2.

101 | Active Listening

Focus: Youth practice active listening skills with each other.

Developmental Assets Tie-in:

2—Positive Family Communication
33—Interpersonal Competence

You will need:

• chalkboard and chalk (or newsprint and markers)

Activity: Explain that people are more willing to form relationships when they feel they're not being judged and someone really cares about them. Dr. Thomas Gordon, author of *Parent Effectiveness Training: The Proven Program for Raising Responsible Children* (New York: Three Rivers Press, 2000), offers a number of relationship-building tips based on what he calls "active listening." Write these on a chalkboard or newsprint:

- Use "I" messages instead of "you" messages (for example, "I feel sad," "I like your approach," "I hear you saying you're angry").

- Encourage the person to speak by responding with "Tell me more" or "How did you feel when that happened?"

- Name feelings that the person is trying to express. "That made you angry" or "You're sad that he broke up with you."

- Listen with empathy.

Ask youth to form teams of three. Ask each team to choose a topic about which they have strong feelings. (Examples could include abortion, gambling, the death penalty, population, global warming.) Have two people in each team practice active listening skills. Ask them to discuss their chosen topics while the third person observes and responds at the end of the exchange by telling them what they did well and what could be improved. Repeat the activity two more times so youth each have a chance to be an observer.

Discussion Questions:

- *What are some things that happened when you tried active listening?*

- *How did it feel to try these techniques? Was it awkward? Helpful?*

- *If these techniques became natural to you, what benefits would you see in using them with other people?*

- *In addition to active listening, what are other ways you can build relationships with people?*

102 | Media Review

Focus: Youth analyze media messages about friendship.

Developmental Assets Tie-in:

15—Positive Peer Influence
33—Interpersonal Competence

Activity: Form seven teams equal in size. Ask each team to discuss one of these media: movies and videos, the Internet, broadcast television, cable television, radio, newspapers, and magazines. (If your group is small, form fewer teams and eliminate some of the types of media.) Have team members discuss the messages their designated medium gives about having friends who model responsible behavior.

Have each team report on its discussion to the larger group. Then as a group, rank the seven media from the one offering the most messages about positive friends to the one offering the fewest messages about positive friends.

Discussion Questions:

- *What types of messages about friends are most common?*

- *Are the messages mostly positive or negative?*

- *Do the media's messages about friends fit with your own experiences? In what ways are they similar and different?*

- *In what ways have you seen friends be positive influences on others? How can you be a positive influence on your friends?*

103 | Listen to Me!

Everyone appreciates a caring listener. You can learn to be a great one! Think about your listening skills and how you can make them even better. Read the examples below and write what you might say in response to a friend who has turned to you to listen.

Developmental Assets Tie-in:

2—Positive Family Communication
15—Positive Peer Influence
33—Interpersonal Competence

1 If you can't give your undivided attention to your friend when he needs to talk *now*, find another time when the two of you can sit down together and carry through with your plans.

I NEED TO DO THIS MORE OFTEN   **I USUALLY DO THIS**
When I don't have time to listen *right now* to a friend, I say:

2 Sometimes people just want to express their feelings to someone they trust, so listen carefully while your friend is talking and resist the urge to share your opinions unless your friend asks you for advice.

I NEED TO DO THIS MORE OFTEN   **I USUALLY DO THIS**
When my friend is done talking, I might say:

3 Pay attention to your friend's body language: how she's sitting, what she's doing with her hands and feet, her tone of voice, and where she's looking. Try to observe the feelings behind her words.

I NEED TO DO THIS MORE OFTEN   **I USUALLY DO THIS**
While I'm paying attention to my friend's body language, here's what I might say:

4 Restate what your friend has said to make sure you understand where he's coming from—
"It sounds to me like . . . So what you're saying is . . ."

I NEED TO DO THIS MORE OFTEN   **I USUALLY DO THIS**
I might also say something like:

104 | Evolving Role Play

Focus: Youth role-play the effects of three different parenting styles.

Developmental Assets Tie-in:

11—Family Boundaries

You will need:

• 3x5 note cards—at least one per youth

Activity: Ask three youth to be volunteers. Have one pretend to be a teenager whose parents need to know every detail about where the teenager goes, what he or she does, and with whom he or she spends time. Have another volunteer be a teenager whose parents seem not to care about these things. The third volunteer should pretend to be a teenager whose parents want to know what the teenager does but aren't overly protective.

Give each of the other youth one 3x5 card. Explain that those who are watching the role play can give one of the players an idea of things to do during the role play that would fit their assigned role. For example, a youth might slip a note that says "act really defensive" to the volunteer who has overprotective parents or "brag about your freedom" to the volunteer whose parents don't seem to care.

Have the volunteers begin by acting out a scene such as this: Three friends get together on a weeknight to have some ice cream. The friend with the permissive parents wants the other two to go to an 11 p.m. movie with her or him.

Then have the role play begin. Encourage youth to give the volunteers ideas throughout the role play.

Discussion Questions:

• Which of the three characters could you most identify with? Why?

• What are the advantages of each of the teenager's situations? The disadvantages?

• What are ways that each of these characters could improve her or his situation?

• Is it important for parents to know where their teenagers are, what they are doing, and who they are with? Why?

My Idea: "Do the activity with volunteers role-playing different types of parents."
— Loran J. Thompson, San Diego, California

105 | Talking about School

Focus: Youth identify ways they can get their parents involved in their education.

Developmental Assets Tie-in:

1—Family Support
2—Positive Family Communication
6—Parent Involvement in Schooling

You will need:

• chalkboard and chalk (or newsprint and markers)

Activity: Have youth brainstorm various topics of conversations about school and then write them on a chalkboard or newsprint. Topics could include homework and projects, school activities, teachers, friends, parent-teacher conferences, your future education plans, school issues, your worries about school, and so on.

Have youth create small groups of three to four people. Evenly divide the conversation topics among the groups; then have the groups identify creative, meaningful ways they could discuss these topics with their parents at home.

Discussion Questions:

• What ideas did your group come up with that you really liked?

• Even though you're becoming more independent from your parents, why is it important to still talk with them about what's going on at school?

• How can you connect with your parents (or other trusted adults) in ways that are more meaningful?

Developmental Assets Tie-in:

1—Family Support
2—Positive Family Communication

Even in the most caring families, some topics are more difficult to discuss than others. At the bottom of this page is a list of words. Write those words in the chart below, either under the category of "Easy to Talk about in My Family" or "Difficult to Talk about in My Family," according to your family dynamics. Once you finish, look at your two lists. Overall, do you feel good about the number of topics you can easily talk about in your family? How can you raise difficult issues?

Easy to Talk about in My Family	Difficult to Talk about in My Family

money

friends

dating

career

future plans

sex

drugs

mistakes

accidents

the family car

extracurricular activities

conflict

video games

the state of your bedroom

time spent as a family

television use

peer pressure

hopes and dreams

curfew

family tension

parties

computer use

movies

politics

music

staying home alone

homework

household chores

favors

time stress

fashion

social injustice

crime

race relations

religion

grades

phone use

privacy

8
Developing Character

Holding strong, positive values is an important
foundation upon which healthy choices are
made. Empathy, personal convictions, and
commitments to the welfare of others shape the
kinds of people we become. The activities in this
chapter are designed to build character in young
people and to help them determine their values
and convictions.

107	# Helping Hands

Focus: Youth discuss ways they have helped others and have been helped by others.

Developmental Assets Tie-in:

9—Service to Others
26—Caring

You will need:

• three or four pieces of colored construction paper for each youth

• markers or pens

Activity: Give each youth three or four pieces of colored construction paper. Have them trace their hands on the paper and then cut out as many hands as they can. On some hands, have youth write about recent incidents when they helped someone else. On the other hands have youth write about incidents when they appreciated help from someone else.

After youth finish, have them describe some of what they wrote. Then work together to hang the hands on a wall in the form of a collage.

Discussion Questions:

• *What are some of the most positive experiences you've had helping or caring for someone? What did you learn from those experiences?*

• *What feelings do you get when someone helps you and cares for you?*

• *What is your favorite memory of someone helping you?*

• *Sometimes we get so preoccupied that we don't think about helping others. What can we do to remember the value of helping and caring for others?*

My Idea: *"Recent incidents when they helped someone else can be on green paper; incidents when they appreciated help from someone else can be on blue paper. The hands can be put together to create a globe of the world."*
—Marilyn Peplau, New Richmond, Wisconsin

108	# Caring for Others

Focus: Youth identify and prepare to do a caring project.

Developmental Assets Tie-in:

9—Service to Others
26—Caring

You will need:

• one sheet of paper for each group of four youth

Activity: On each sheet of paper, write one group or issue that would benefit from the help of youth volunteers, such as the environment, elderly people, animals, children, families, or singles. Have youth form teams of four; then give each team a sheet of paper. Ask each team to identify three caring projects they could do that would help this group of people or cause. For example, youth could pick up trash in a community park one weekend day. They could take a group of younger children swinging and sliding for an hour. Youth who can drive could run some errands for an elderly person.

Once youth finish selecting projects, have the teams report back to the whole group. Have the group discuss whether they want to do one larger project or form smaller teams to do a number of projects. Set goals for doing these projects.

Discussion Questions:

• *What are some reasons you selected the project or projects that you did?*

• *What are the most important things to consider when planning a helping project?*

• *In addition to the service you will provide, what else might you expect to learn or gain from doing this project?*

109 | Say It on a Screen Saver

Developmental Assets Tie-in:

26—Caring
27—Equality and Social Justice
28—Integrity
29—Honesty
30—Responsibility
31—Restraint

When the monitor of the computer you are using goes to screen saver mode, what are you looking at? What screen savers have you noticed on other people's monitors? Think of a screen saver message and graphics that would remind you and others who see it of one of the six Positive Values assets. Choose one you think is especially important and design your screen saver here. Then, if you can, install it! Some examples might include "Let your values guide you," "Positive values matter," or "Create a caring world."

If you need a refresher, the six Positive Values assets are:

Asset 26: Caring—Young person places high value on helping other people.

Asset 27: Equality and Social Justice—Young person places high value on promoting equality and reducing hunger and poverty.

Asset 28: Integrity—Young person acts on convictions and stands up for her or his beliefs.

Asset 29: Honesty—Young person "tells the truth even when it is not easy."

Asset 30: Responsibility—Young person accepts and takes personal responsibility.

Asset 31: Restraint—Young person believes it is important not to be sexually active or to use alcohol or other drugs.

110 | Random Acts of Kindness

Focus: Youth explore the practice of caring as its own reward.

Developmental Assets Tie-in:

26—Caring
33—Interpersonal Competence
38—Self-Esteem

You will need:

• index cards or shared computer file

• newsprint and markers (or chalkboard and chalk)

Note:

This activity will take more than one session.

Activity: Write the phrase "Random Acts of Kindness" on a chalkboard or newsprint; then ask the group what this phrase means to them. Have them give examples of kind acts that they have done (or observed) and that others have done for them.

Brainstorm a list of simple, random acts of kindness (such as holding doors open for strangers, helping a sibling with homework, leaving money in a community donation box). Set a goal for the total number of acts that the group wants to accomplish. Tell youth that they will work in pairs to perform anonymous acts of caring for one week. Decide on how to record what was done—pairs could write each act on an index card or record them in a shared computer file or on a common Web site. Suggest that youth keep a journal to record reactions to the kind acts they performed.

A week later, report the total number of kind acts and celebrate reaching the goal.

Discussion Questions:

• What kinds of things did you do? Why?

• Which were the most fun? Which made you feel most satisfied?

• Were there any that you wish that you hadn't done?

• Were you able to observe any people as they discovered your random acts of kindness? If so, how did they react?

• What did you learn about yourselves as you performed your random acts of kindness? What did you learn about others?

• Why is it important to do random acts of kindness?

Bonus Idea: If you have time, consider showing the movie *Pay It Forward* (rated PG-13) before the youth perform their random acts of kindness.

111 | Pictures of Injustice

Focus: Youth respond to pictures that represent injustice.

Developmental Assets Tie-in:

27—Equality and Social Justice
34—Cultural Competence

You will need:

• five magazine or newspaper photos that depict injustice

• five sticky notes (or Post-it Notes) for each youth

Activity: Find five magazine or newspaper photographs that illustrate injustice (both domestic and international) and hang them around the room. For example, find pictures that show poverty, acts of violence, acts of discrimination, and so on.

Give each youth five removable adhesive notes (such as Post-it Notes). Ask youth to write on separate adhesive notes a one-sentence response to each picture and then have them post their sentence near each photograph. Encourage youth to remain silent while they do this activity.

Give everyone time to go back and read what others wrote.

Discussion Questions:

• How did you feel when you looked at these photographs?

• Which photograph had the most impact on you? Why?

• What did you think about what other people wrote?

• Did you want to do something about what you saw? What can you do?

• How do you feel about injustice?

That's Not Fair!

When it comes to social justice, the United States has made a lot of progress in some areas, but lags in others. Check your opinion on each of the issues below. Feel free to check as many different answers as you feel apply to each situation.

Developmental Assets Tie-in:

27—Equality and Social Justice
34—Cultural Competence

Issues	I am really concerned about this.	We've made a lot of progress in this area.	We still have a lot of work to do.	This injustice is not as serious as it sounds.
1. Racial discrimination	☐	☐	☐	☐
2. Gender discrimination	☐	☐	☐	☐
3. Poverty	☐	☐	☐	☐
4. Sexual orientation discrimination	☐	☐	☐	☐
5. Hunger	☐	☐	☐	☐
6. Ethnic/cultural discrimination	☐	☐	☐	☐
7. Religious discrimination	☐	☐	☐	☐
8. Age discrimination	☐	☐	☐	☐
9. Disability discrimination	☐	☐	☐	☐
10. Social class discrimination	☐	☐	☐	☐

113 | Opinions Count

Focus: Youth assert their beliefs by writing a letter to a newspaper, magazine, or online forum.

Developmental Assets Tie-in:

8—Youth as Resources
28—Integrity

You will need:

• writing paper

• pens

Activity: Explain that one way to stand up for what you believe is to speak out. Encourage youth to choose a movie, TV show, magazine article, newspaper article, or other media story about which they have a strong opinion. They may either agree or disagree with the story or its presentation.

Help youth find out to whom they should address the letter. Then work with youth in crafting a respectful but provocative letter that expresses their opinion. Encourage youth to use "I" statements and be specific about their concerns. (See activity 101 on page 98 for ideas.)

Ask for volunteers to read aloud what they wrote before they mail their letters. Youth can choose to send their comments to the local newspaper (or school paper) as a letter to the editor (especially if the story they're writing about recently happened), or they can send their letter to the author, editor, or producer of the story. If some of the letters are published, display them prominently in your classroom or meeting area.

Discussion Questions:

• *On what topics are you most likely to take a stand? Why?*

• *What is the hardest part about expressing your beliefs?*

• *What are some things you can do to help you be assertive?*

Bonus Idea: Follow a current issue that is happening in your community. Have youth write letters to the editor or an opinion piece for your local newspaper. Monitor what happens over time.

114 | Classroom Continuum

Focus: Youth stand on a continuum, based on their own experiences of being assertive.

Developmental Assets Tie-in:

8—Youth as Resources
28—Integrity

You will need:

• masking tape

• two sheets of paper

• a marker

Activity: Put a piece of masking tape on the floor of your classroom or meeting room. The tape should stretch from one end of the room to the other. At one end, hang a sign that says "Agree." On the opposite end, hang a sign that says "Disagree."

Tell youth that you're going to read a series of statements. After each statement, they should move to a place along the continuum that best reflects their true experiences. Encourage youth to be honest about what really happens, not what they wish would happen.

Read statements such as these (or others that fit):

• When someone says something I disagree with, I tell that person how I feel.

• I talk through issues with somebody before making a decision.

• When someone hurts me, I tell the person.

• When a clerk gives me too much change, I tell the clerk.

• It's easier for me to state my opinion around strangers than around friends or family.

• I feel my family accepts me when I have a differing opinion.

• I often compare viewpoints on subjects with my friends.

• I find it easy to stand up for what I believe.

Discussion Questions:

• *Did you find yourself more often agreeing or disagreeing with the statements I read? Or were you in the middle a lot?*

• *When is it most important to be assertive? Can you share any examples? When is it least important?*

• *If a friend is having a hard time asserting her or his beliefs or choices, how can you help her or him be more assertive?*

115 | Values

People are always talking about "values." You may hear the word used by family, friends, and the media, but what does it mean?

Think of all the places where you spend time. What are the beliefs that guide your actions in these places? What motivates others to act a certain way in these places? Choose three values that are important to you no matter where you are. Choose from the ones that are given below, or write your own.

Developmental Assets Tie-in:

26—Caring
27—Equality and Social Justice
28—Integrity
29—Honesty
30—Responsibility
31—Restraint

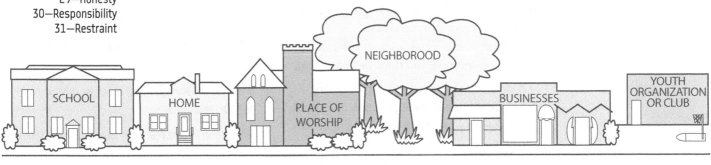

Consider the feelings of others.

Tell the truth.

Help without being asked.

Stand up for what you believe.

Do what you promise to do.

Care for the needs of others.

Have faith.

Advocate for the less fortunate.

Drug-free is the best way to be.

Finish what you start.

Family first.

Stick by your friends.

Be responsible.

Save sexual intercourse for adulthood.

Stay sober.

Promote equality.

Act on your convictions.

Be yourself. Don't follow the crowd.

116 | Fudging the Truth

Focus: Youth discuss small lies.

Developmental Assets Tie-in:

29—Honesty

You will need:

• a chalkboard and chalk (or newsprint and a marker)

Activity: Have youth get into groups of three or four. Say: "Telling the truth gets trickier when we know it might hurt someone's feelings. It's often easier to tell small lies when we want to be polite."

Explain that youth are to discuss within their groups what they would do in each of the situations you list on the chalkboard or newsprint. List situations such as these:

- A friend who is upset because he's gained weight asks you if you think he's gotten fat.
- A classmate has been making a pottery bowl and has redone it 10 times. It still looks crooked to you, and she wants to know if you think it's now straight.
- A friend bought a new jacket that he just loves. You think it looks awful. Your friend wants to know what you think.
- A relative you like gives you a sweater for a gift. It fits, but you really don't like the style.

Discussion Questions:

- *How difficult is it to tell the truth in these situations? Why?*
- *Do you always tell the truth? Why or why not?*
- *Is it easier for you to be honest with some people than others? Why?*
- *If you value honesty does it mean you should never lie? Why or why not?*
- *What if you lie and feel guilty about it? What should you do?*
- *What does it mean to value honesty?*

117 | Taking Charge

Focus: Youth role-play responsibility.

Developmental Assets Tie-in:

30—Responsibility

You will need:

• several sections of newspaper

Activity: Ask for four volunteers to participate in a role play; then take them aside to explain what they'll be doing. Make sure the other group members cannot hear what you're saying.

First explain the difference between accepting responsibility and taking responsibility: "When you *accept* responsibility, you're saying 'yes' to a task, and when you *take* responsibility you actually follow through with that task." Then ask one youth to refuse to accept and take responsibility; another to refuse to accept responsibility but then take responsibility after the fact; a third youth to accept responsibility but then not act on it; and the last youth to accept and also act on being responsible. Explain that you want the four volunteers to stand in front of the group, wad up newspapers, and throw them all around the room. Tell them that when you ask them a question, you want them to answer in a way that fits with their assigned role. Say that you also want the two who are to take responsibility to clean up the mess after you leave.

Give them time to make a mess. After a while, say: "What a mess! Who's going to accept responsibility and clean this up?" Allow each youth to answer. Say: "Well, I want you all to clean this up." Then walk away while two of the youth clean it up.

Discussion Questions:

- *Who took the most responsibility? How?*
- *Who took the least responsibility?*
- *What are important aspects of personal responsibility? Why?*
- *What gets in the way of your accepting and taking responsibility?*
- *In which areas of your life would you like to accept and take more responsibility? Why?*
- *Which person did you have the most respect for in this situation? The least amount of respect? Why?*

You can accept and take responsibility in all areas of your life. Complete each of the statements below, naming at least one way you can take responsibility in each area.

Developmental Assets Tie-in:

30—Responsibility

I can take more responsibility at home by:

_____

_____

I can take more responsibility at school by:

_____

_____

I can take more responsibility in my community by:

_____

_____

I can take more responsibility with my friends by:

_____

_____

I can take more responsibility with my personal goals by:

_____

_____

119 | To Tell the Truth

Focus: Youth debate whether a lie can ever be the best course of action.

Developmental Assets Tie-in:

28—Integrity
29—Honesty

You will need:

• crepe paper (three to four rolls per team, in two colors)

• marker

• newsprint

• one die

• tape

• a coin

Activity: Print this statement on a sheet of newsprint in large letters: "Honesty is not always the best policy." Form two teams by asking each youth to roll the die. Those who roll from one to three are on one team, and those who roll from four to six are on the other (teams don't have to be equal in size).

Give each team a roll of crepe paper and tell them to use it to create some form of "team uniform." Each team member must wear the team color.

Post the chart that displays the statement of debate. Ask one team to defend this statement, thinking of reasons and examples to prove why it is good advice. Assign the other team to argue against this statement, thinking of reasons and examples to prove why it is bad advice.

Give teams time to prepare their arguments and decide who will be first speakers and second speakers for their teams.

Use a coin toss to determine which team will go first. Listen to both first speakers, then both second speakers. Time carefully so that each speaker gets only two minutes.

Discussion Questions:

• Is there a difference between "withholding the truth" and "telling a lie"? Why or why not?

• If a 10-year-old child asked you if it's ever okay to tell a lie, what would you say? Are there different degrees of honesty (for example, lying to spare someone's feelings)?

• Why is honesty one of the 40 Developmental Assets?

• How important is honesty for the welfare of a society or a community?

120 | What the Media Says

Focus: Youth analyze messages about sex, alcohol, and other drugs in the media.

Developmental Assets Tie-in:

31—Restraint
35—Resistance Skills

You will need:

• magazines

Activity: Choose magazines that are popular with teenagers. Younger teenagers tend to like magazines that are geared toward teens. Older teenagers tend to prefer general-interest magazines, such as *Rolling Stone*, *Glamour*, and *People*. Ask youth to look through the magazine articles and advertisements in regard to messages about sex, alcohol, and drugs.

Discussion Questions:

• What does this magazine say about sex, alcohol, or other drugs?

• How typical is this message compared to other messages you read or hear?

• How much do you think your friends agree with this message? Why?

• How much does the media influence your values about sex, alcohol, or other drugs?

• Do females and males get different messages about sex, alcohol, and other drugs? Why do you think this is the case?

• Many people believe it is important for teenagers to abstain from sex, alcohol, and other drugs. What are reasons for this perspective?

• Why do many teenagers choose to abstain from sex, alcohol, and other drugs? Why do others choose to get involved with sex, alcohol, or other drugs?

• Do you think it's important for teenagers to value abstaining from sex, alcohol, and other drugs? Why?

• How can youth support each other in choosing to abstain?

The asset of restraint says it's better for teenagers to wait until they're adults to have sexual intercourse, to use alcohol responsibly at the legal age, and never to use other drugs. Under each category, list three reasons why you think it's important for teenagers to have restraint in these areas.

Developmental Assets Tie-in:

31—Restraint
35—Resistance Skills

Three reasons to abstain from sexual activity as a teenager:

1 _____

2 _____

3 _____

Three reasons to not drink alcohol as a teenager:

1 _____

2 _____

3 _____

Three reasons to not use other drugs at all:

1 _____

2 _____

3 _____

122 | Random Acts of Service

Focus: Youth choose simple ways to serve others.

Developmental Assets Tie-in:

9—Service to Others
26—Caring

You will need:

• chalkboard and chalk (or newsprint and a marker)

Note:

This activity will take more than one session.

Activity: Have youth brainstorm a list of simple, easy ways to serve others. Write all the ideas on a chalkboard or newsprint. Examples might include taking out the garbage, shoveling a snowy walk, mowing someone's lawn, writing a thinking-of-you note to someone, or sending a coupon for ice cream or a movie to a child.

Then have each young person choose one thing they could do within the next week (either anonymously or not). Have them observe the receiver's reactions and also notice their own reaction to the receiver's reactions.

The next time you meet together, ask youth to share their experiences with the group.

Discussion Questions:

• Which activity did you choose? Why?

• How did you feel while you were doing the activity?

• How did you feel after completing the activity?

• How did the receiver's reaction affect your feelings about service?

• Do you want to do other acts of service? Why or why not?

My Idea: *"We do this as a whole conference activity with our youth leadership conference of more than 350 youth and adults. The youth love it, and they enjoy sharing all the ways they came up with to be a servant leader."*

—Jessica Andrews, Lawrenceville, Georgia

123 | Building Assets in Other Young People

Focus: Youth choose simple ways to build assets in others.

Developmental Assets Tie-in:

The Developmental Assets Framework

You will need:

• chalkboard and chalk (or newsprint and a marker)

• a photocopy of the Developmental Assets among Youth list from page 18 for each young person

Activity: Distribute photocopies of the Developmental Assets list from page 18 for each young person so that they can become more familiar with the Developmental Assets framework.

As a group, brainstorm simple ways to build assets in young people at school, in your organization, or in your community. For example, young people may decide to focus on a specific asset type (such as support) and:

• Call people by name and smile at them when they're walking in the hallway from class to class.

• Create asset posters to hang around your school, organization, or community.

• Make bookmarks focusing on some of the assets and distribute them through your school and community libraries.

• Form a committee to work with the student council, your community's continuing education, or the decision-making board of your organization to suggest ways to build assets in children and youth.

After you brainstorm a list of at least 10 ideas, choose one to implement. Focus on making your idea simple and doable. (You can always do more later if the first idea goes well.) Then create a timeline and a plan, and have young people work together to transform the idea into reality.

Discussion Questions:

• Which activity did you choose? Why?

• How did you feel while you were doing the activity? Why?

• How did you feel after completing the activity? Why?

• What other assets could we build?

My Idea: *"We made videos—skits—of the assets and presented them to the school."*

—Loran J. Thompson, San Diego, California

Choose a kind of service you would like to do (for example, mowing a neighbor's lawn, baby-sitting so the parents can run errands, or cleaning up litter from your block) and how much time you can realistically spend doing it. Then fill in the contract below. Consider showing or giving the contract to the person you plan to help.

Developmental Assets Tie-in:

9—Service to Others
26—Caring

CONTRACT FOR SERVICE

I, _____ (your name), make a

commitment to _____

_____ (type of service).

This service will be of help to _____

_____ (name of receiver)

because _____

_____ (reason for doing the project).

I realistically can spend about _____ hours on this project.

I intend to start by _____ (date).

_____   _____
(your signature)   (today's date)

9
Promoting Diversity

Our world is becoming more and more diverse, and young people need to develop the skills that will help them build relationships with all kinds of people—people who are like them and people who are not. This chapter includes activities and ready-to-use handouts that young people can do to become more comfortable—and more skilled in their relationships—with other people.

| 125 | # Different Books for Different Folks |

Focus: Youth think about exploring different types of reading.

Developmental Assets Tie-in:

25—Reading for Pleasure
34—Cultural Competence

You will need:

• comic books

• magazines

• classic literature, such as *Jane Eyre* or *Oliver Twist*

• modern literature, such as a book from the *Harry Potter* series or a John Grisham mystery

• nonfiction, such as a biography or history book

Activity: Spread the books and magazines across a table or on the floor. Give youth a few minutes to browse through the books and magazines and pick up one they would really like to read. Then have them form pairs and tell their partners about the book or magazine they chose—why they want to read what they selected or why they might recommend it to someone else.

Discussion Questions:

• *What did you choose for yourself? Why did you choose it?*

• *How did you choose your reading material? Did you go by its title, its cover art, the description on the back, or by the quoted review comments?*

• *Are you willing to try reading a book that you wouldn't normally buy or check out of the library? If so, why? If not, why not?*

• *Why is it important to read a wide variety of books and magazines?*

| 126 | # Conversation Circles |

Focus: Youth express their opinions on statements about cultural competence.

Developmental Assets Tie-in:

33—Interpersonal Competence
34—Cultural Competence

You will need:

• overhead projector and transparencies if your group is quite large

Activity: Ask youth to form two circles, one inside the other, with an equal number of people. Spread out to leave plenty of space between people in the circles. Have youth in the inner circle turn and face youth in the outer circle, forming conversation pairs. After you read a statement, have the young people in each pair tell each other whether they agree or disagree with it and why. After the discussion of each statement, youth in the outer circle will move one person clockwise to form new pairs for the next statement.

Use the below statements, allowing time for each partner discussion. (If your group is very large and it will be difficult for youth to hear the statements, write them on an overhead transparency and project them onto a screen.)

• Our cultural heritage is important to my family.

• If people take the time to learn more about different races or cultures, they will be less likely to fear them.

• I enjoy learning about my friends' racial or cultural backgrounds.

• My neighborhood does a good job of welcoming people who have come from other countries.

• My school doesn't have a lot of tension between racial, ethnic, or cultural groups.

• My teachers have helped me learn about different cultures and traditions.

Discussion Questions:

• *What did you hear that was surprising? What did you hear that was reassuring? What did you hear that felt like a personal challenge to you?*

• *Were there any differences in opinion? How did you handle that?*

• *Which statements did you agree with most strongly? Which statements did you disagree with most strongly?*

• *Did your discussions uncover any improvements that you would like to make in your community or school? If so, what are they? How can our group help to start these improvements?*

How much contact do you have with people of other races, ethnic backgrounds, and cultures? In the inventory below, check the amount of contact you have had.

Developmental Assets Tie-in:

34—Cultural Competence

TYPE OF CONTACT	OFTEN	ONCE IN A WHILE	NEVER
See people with cultural backgrounds that are different from mine in my community	❏	❏	❏
Talk to people with cultural backgrounds that are different from mine	❏	❏	❏
See television shows that positively portray people with a variety of cultural backgrounds	❏	❏	❏
Listen to music from other cultures	❏	❏	❏
Hear others talk positively about people from a variety of cultures	❏	❏	❏
Eat foods from other cultures	❏	❏	❏
Study in school about people with a variety of cultural backgrounds	❏	❏	❏
Read positive stories about people from many cultures	❏	❏	❏
Attend cross-cultural events	❏	❏	❏

Focus: Youth share their own experiences of being included and excluded.

Developmental Assets Tie-in:

33—Interpersonal Competence
36—Peaceful Conflict Resolution

Activity: Have youth stand in a circle and hold hands. Start by reading each of the following statements, and then add others that will make the activity meaningful for your community. If a statement is true in the life of one of the young people, he or she will place one foot either inside or outside the circle, depending on your instructions. Have youth step back to the circle after each statement.

- If you have ever felt that you were being treated unfairly because of your gender, place your foot outside the circle.

- If you have ever felt welcomed by a group of people you didn't know, place your foot inside the circle.

- If you have ever felt afraid for your safety because of your race, place your foot outside the circle.

- If you have a friend who has a cultural, racial, or ethnic background that is different from yours, place your foot inside the circle.

- If you speak more than one language, place your foot inside the circle.

- If you have ever felt that you were being treated unfairly because of your accent or the language you speak, place your foot outside the circle.

- If you have ever felt that you were being treated unfairly because of the shape or size of your body or because you have a disability, place your foot outside the circle.

- If you have ever felt embarrassed by the way your parent(s) or guardian(s) look, speak, or act, place your foot outside the circle.

- If you have ever felt at home in someone else's faith community, place your foot inside the circle.

- If you have ever introduced yourself to someone you didn't know, place your foot inside the circle.

Discussion Questions:

- What surprised you about this activity?

- What part of this activity made you feel uncomfortable or sad?

- What questions would you like to ask each other about your responses? (Allow plenty of time for this question.)

- How can we help each other feel more included?

Diversity. It's all around us. Using the following list of different types of diversity, answer the questions below.

Developmental Assets Tie-in:

34—Cultural Competence

- Ethnic and racial diversity
- Age diversity
- Political diversity
- Physical ability diversity
- Social ability diversity
- Other types of diversity

- Economic diversity
- Gender diversity
- Religious diversity
- Mental ability diversity
- Sexual orientation diversity

Which kind of diversity are you most familiar with?

Which kind of diversity do you have the least experience with?

Which kind of diversity is creating tension in your community?

Which kind of diversity does our world need? Why?

| # Out vs. In

Focus: Youth play a game that illustrates exclusivity and inclusiveness.

Developmental Assets Tie-in:

34—Cultural Competence

Activity: Have youth form a circle. Ask young people who are right-handed to stay in the circle and all the left-handed youth to leave the circle.

Have the right-handed circle members lock arms tightly. Explain that the object of this activity is for the outsiders to try to break into the circle. If someone succeeds, he or she joins the group and then chooses someone within the circle to leave.

After doing the activity for a while, ask:

• How did it feel to be part of the circle and try hard not to let others in? Why?

• How did it feel to be an outsider? Why?

• How did it feel to be part of the circle and then be asked to leave without any apparent reason?

Repeat the activity. This time have all the brown-eyed youth form a circle and hold hands. Have all the other youth stand outside the circle. Explain that when someone from the outside wants to join the circle, he or she should gently tap the shoulder of someone in the circle and ask to join in. Whenever those in the circle are asked, they are to open up their arms and let the people in.

Feel free to adapt this activity depending on how personally you want youth to experience discrimination. If you wish, you can single out youth in a more neutral way, such as by having some volunteers wear a red bandana.

Discussion Questions:

• How did you feel about this activity compared to the first activity? Why?

• Why is it good to get to know people who are different from us?

• What one thing can you do to expand the circle of people you know and with whom you feel comfortable?

Bonus Idea: If you wish to go deeper with this experience, get the study guide that accompanies Jane Elliott's Blue Eyes/Brown Eyes exercise at www.newsreel.org/guides/blueeyed.htm.

My Idea: *"I give this activity a 'best' rating. I use lots of activities like these with at-risk youth."*

—Janece Wooley-Woulard, Toledo, Ohio

| # Diverse Role Models

Focus: Youth study the religious involvement of role models.

Developmental Assets Tie-in:

14—Adult Role Models
19—Religious Community

Activity: Have youth identify role models who make or have made the world a better place. They may mention Nobel Peace Prize winners, Dr. Martin Luther King Jr., Rumi, Gandhi, Mother Teresa, the Dalai Lama, or more local examples.

Ask youth to form teams of three. Have each team discuss what they know about one role model and that person's involvement in religion. (If time allows, provide reference books or access to the Internet for research.)

Discussion Questions:

• Of the role models we've named, how involved are they in religion? What impact does that involvement seem to have on them?

• Does learning about role models' religious involvement change your view of them? Why or why not?

• Is religious involvement usually positive or negative? Why?

• Is it important to know a person's religious involvement before deciding whether to look up to her or him? Why or why not?

• The principle of separation of church and state, which forbids the government from endorsing or promoting religion, can be found in the U.S. Constitution. How do you feel when leaders make political decisions based on their religious beliefs?

• How important is religious involvement to you? Why?

Think about the experiences you've had with religious organizations. Briefly write about one negative experience and one positive experience. Then write about your current feelings about your involvement (if any) in a religious organization and how—if at all—you'd like that to change.

Developmental Assets Tie-in:

19—Religious Community
34—Cultural Competence

My most positive experience with a religious organization was:

My most negative experience with a religious organization was:

About my current level of involvement, I feel:

Focus: Youth investigate demographics in their community.

Developmental Assets Tie-in:

34—Cultural Competence

You will need:

• demographic data for your community (Census data is available through your city, county, or township office or the reference desk at the library. United States census information is available at www.census. gov; the link to "State and County Quick Facts" is especially helpful.)

• markers

• newsprint

• reference materials

Note:

This activity may take more than one session.

Before the group arrives: Make copies of current, local census data for youth to review. Make sure to include information about population growth (or loss) and the ethnic makeup of your community or neighborhood. Bring this key data for 30 years ago and 50 years ago as well. If you would like to expand this activity, invite a person who works with immigrants in your community to join you for this session to talk about services your community provides to newcomers from other countries.

Activity: Give time for youth to look through the census data you have provided. As a group, discuss interesting or surprising information that they discovered. List where the newcomers in your community have come from and locate these places on a map or globe. If there are any young people in the group who recently immigrated to the United States, invite them to share their experiences. Ask when each youth's ancestors first came to this country—this is a nation of immigrants!

Compare the current information about population changes with the data from 30 and 50 years ago. Ask youth to offer their theories about why these changes have taken place.

Form teams of three and ask each group to research one of the places that current immigrants in your community have come from and to record five key pieces of information about that place on newsprint to share with the group. Provide reference books or access to the Internet.

Ask each team to present its five key pieces of information.

Discussion Questions:

• *How else could we learn more about different races and ethnicities in our community?*

• *Do you know any recent immigrants? If so, how did you meet each other? What do you have in common? What has been challenging about getting to know each other? (If your group includes recent immigrants, ask them to talk about their experiences of moving into your community and getting to know people.)*

• *What different reactions to newcomers in your community have you observed in other adults and youth? Which seem helpful? Which seem to cause problems? Why do you suppose people respond to newcomers in the ways they do?*

• *How can we help newcomers feel more part of our community?*

134 | Injustice and Me

Developmental Assets Tie-in:

27—Equality and Social Justice
34—Cultural Competence

Have you ever been in a situation in which you were treated unfairly? Have you ever been insensitive or unfair to someone else? Answer each of these items by checking the box that shows how often you have been part of these types of situations. What have these experiences taught you?

How often have you . . .	Never	1–3 times in my life	At least once a month
Been discriminated against because of your race?	☐	☐	☐
Made an unfair assumption about someone because of her or his race?	☐	☐	☐
Been mistreated because of your gender?	☐	☐	☐
Treated someone else unfairly because of her or his gender?	☐	☐	☐
Been stereotyped because of your age?	☐	☐	☐
Disrespected someone because of his or her age?	☐	☐	☐
Been misunderstood because of your religious beliefs?	☐	☐	☐
Treated someone else unfairly because of her or his religious beliefs?	☐	☐	☐
Been looked down on because you were poor?	☐	☐	☐
Looked down on someone because he or she is poor?	☐	☐	☐
Been mistreated because of the way you look?	☐	☐	☐
Mistreated someone because of how he or she looks?	☐	☐	☐

135 | Golden Nuggets

Focus: Youth discuss how valued they are in society and in their community.

Developmental Assets Tie-in:

7—Community Values Youth
8—Youth as Resources
34—Cultural Competence
38—Self-Esteem

You will need:

• rocks of different sizes and shapes—one for each youth

Activity: Have youth sit in groups of four. Give each of them a rock, and then ask everyone to compare rocks and decide which one is the most valuable and which is the least valuable. Then have them lay the rocks in a line that shows the order of importance. Have groups share how they determined which rocks were most valuable and why.

Then have the young people pick up their original rocks. Tell them that each rock has gold inside, and each nugget of gold inside is unique. Have them again lay the rocks in a line that shows the order of importance.

Discussion Questions:

• Was it more difficult to determine the value of the rocks based on what you could see on the outside or based on what you couldn't see on the inside? Why?

• In terms of judging people, how do we usually decide who's valuable and who's not? Are those the best ways to determine these things? Why or why not?

• Think about all the age groups in our society. Which age groups are most valued? Least valued? Why?

• Overall, does our community place enough value on youth?

• Are youth in our community more likely to be viewed as valuable for what they are now, or for what they might become?

• What would you suggest needs to happen to encourage our community to value youth more?

• What steps can you take to ensure that young people are valued?

136 | Fair or Unfair?

Focus: Youth experience and discuss inequality.

Developmental Assets Tie-in:

7—Community Values Youth
27—Equality and Social Justice
34—Cultural Competence

You will need:

• a deck of playing cards

Activity: Have everyone sit in a circle so they can all see each other. Give each person a card from the deck; then have everyone turn over their card to display it in front of them.

Explain that anyone with a jack, queen, or king is a rich ruler who owns anyone who has a card with a number on it. The numbered cards tell your value. The lower the number, the lower your value. If you have an ace, you are worth nothing.

Discussion Questions:

• Is this fair? Why or why not?

• How does it feel to be labeled before you do or say anything?

• Have you heard about societies in which this kind of system exists—either in our country or in another country?

• How would you have felt about this activity if we had just stopped after you received the card without discussing your value? Would you have felt better if you had received a higher card than a lower card? Why?

• Why do people label other people? How can we deal with labels?

• What steps can we take to ensure that all people are valued?

Developmental Assets Tie-in:

34—Cultural Competence

Our schools, organizations, and communities are becoming more and more diverse. Show people the boxes below and see which box they sign. Then ask them about that experience. Cultural competence and diversity aren't always apparent. Sometimes you need to ask to find out how culturally rich some people are. Try to find 16 different people to sign the 16 boxes.

Speaks two languages.	Can count to five in another language.	Owns something bought in another country.	Has received a postcard from another country.
Has traveled to another country.	Has lived in another country.	Has dreams of someday living in another country.	Donates money to help people in another country.
Likes food from another country.	Can name a country in Africa, Asia, and South America.	Is friends with someone of a different race or ethnicity.	Has a passport.
Has a friend or family member currently living in another country.	Was born in another country.	Knows someone from a different religious tradition.	Is worried about events in a specific country.

10
Setting Goals, Recognizing Hopes, and Realizing Dreams

Everyone has hopes for the future, but how do they get there? Young people not only need dreams but also the skills to make their dreams come true. This chapter includes practical ways for young people to set goals and envision a future they're excited about.

138 | The Ideal Neighborhood

Focus: Youth think about types of activities for teens in a "perfect" neighborhood.

Developmental Assets Tie-in:

4—Caring Neighborhood
13—Neighborhood Boundaries

You will need:

• large sheets of paper— one for each group

• markers, crayons, or other drawing tools

Activity: Have youth form teams of four (more or less). Give each team a large sheet of paper to draw a perfect neighborhood that is ideal for people of all ages. Encourage the teams to talk about problems and challenges that currently exist in their own neighborhoods that keep them from becoming like the utopian neighborhood they've drawn.

Then have each team show their drawing to the rest of the group while suggesting one or two ideas for how their neighborhood could become more like their picture.

Discussion Questions:

• *What are the most important things to have in an ideal neighborhood?*

• *Which of these things are available in your neighborhood? Why?*

• *Where are the biggest gaps in your neighborhood?*

• *What things can youth do to make their neighborhoods better places to live?*

139 | Inspirational Sayings

Focus: Youth critique sayings about expectations.

Developmental Assets Tie-in:

16—High Expectations
40—Positive View of Personal Future

You will need:

• chalkboard and chalk (or newsprint and a marker)

Activity: Write the following sayings on a chalkboard or newsprint: "Dream Big," "Expect the Best," "You Can Do More than You Think," "Dream Impossible Dreams—and Do Them," and "Be the Best You Can Be."

Have youth form groups of three or four. Explain that groups are to discuss and critique each of the sayings. Have groups discuss questions such as these: Which are realistic? Which are not? What are the problems with any of the sayings? Which offer good advice? Why?

Discussion Questions:

• *Many people like to collect sayings, phrases, and quotes such as these and others. Why?*

• *Do you have any favorite sayings of your own?*

• *Do these sayings inspire you or put too much pressure on you? Why?*

• *How do others inspire you?*

• *How do you inspire yourselves?*

My Idea: *"I love asking young people for their favorite sayings because it gives insight into their personalities, hopes, and lives."*

—Jessica Andrews, Lawrenceville, Georgia

Developmental Assets Tie-in:

16—High Expectations

Do you know what is expected of you? Do you know what others expect you to do and how they expect you to do it? Is enough expected of you—or too much? Think about these questions as you fill in the chart below. Where the expectations aren't clear or aren't at a comfortable level, talk about them with the people mentioned.

	What I expect of myself	What my family expects of me	What my teachers expect of me	What my friends expect of me
Personal values that guide the decisions I make				
Taking care of my own health and safety				
Appropriate behavior				
How I treat others				
What my future will be				
Other expectations				

141 | Redefining Success

Focus: Youth identify ways people search for success and meaning.

Developmental Assets Tie-in:

37—Personal Power
39—Sense of Purpose

You will need:

• chalkboard and chalk (or newsprint and a marker)

Activity: As a group, brainstorm a list of ways people search for success and meaning. Examples might include money, fame, a loving family, achievement, and awards. After you finish, ask:

• Are these things bad? Why or why not?

• What's your idea of success?

• What's difficult about finding meaning in life?

Then read this quote by author Joseph Campbell to the group. "You have a success in life, but then just think of it—what kind of life was it? What good was it that you've never done the thing you wanted to do in all your life? I always tell my students, go where your body and soul want to go. . . . Follow your bliss and don't be afraid, and doors will open where you didn't know they were going to be."

Discussion Questions:

• *How hard is it to find bliss or purpose in life? Why?*

• *What keeps people from finding bliss or purpose?*

• *If I asked you if you knew what your purpose was in life, could you tell me? Why or why not?*

• *What would you need to do to find your purpose?*

142 | A Look to the Future

Focus: Youth create collages representing their futures.

Developmental Assets Tie-in:

39—Sense of Purpose
40—Positive View of Personal Future

You will need:

• a large sheet of paper

• magazines, catalogs, and newspapers

• glue

• scissors

Activity: On a large sheet of paper, have youth create a group collage of what they think the future will look like. Encourage them to cut out pictures and words from magazines, catalogs, and newspapers to glue onto the paper.

After everyone finishes, have them explain their work. Then display their collages.

Discussion Questions:

• *How different do you think your life in the future will be from what it is like now? Why?*

• *What kinds of things do you worry about in the future? What scares you?*

• *What are some things that really give you hope?*

• *How can you prepare for the future so that it will be exciting and positive?*

On August 28, 1963, Martin Luther King Jr. gave his "I Have a Dream" speech in Washington, DC. The message was clear: King was optimistic about the future.

In the space below, write a short message of your dream for the future. Do like Dr. King. Don't get caught up in disturbing events that may surround you.

Dream big. Dream positively. Dream with optimism.

Developmental Assets Tie-in:

39—Sense of Purpose
40—Positive View of Personal Future

144 | Yes! No! Yes!

Focus: Youth identify what gives meaning to their lives (and what doesn't).

Developmental Assets Tie-in:

37—Personal Power
38—Self-Esteem
39—Sense of Purpose
40—Positive View of Personal Future

You will need:

• chalkboard and chalk (or newsprint and markers)

Activity: Have young people form groups of three or four. On a chalkboard or a piece of newsprint, write: What five things make life meaningful to you?

Give groups time to discuss this question. After they finish, have each group report what they learned.

On a chalkboard or a piece of newsprint, write: What five things in life make you want to crawl back into bed and never come out?

Give groups time to discuss this question. After they finish, have the groups report what they learned.

Discussion Questions:

• *What did you discover about what gives your life meaning?*

• *How is that different from the things that make you want to crawl back into bed?*

• *Why does it matter if you know the difference between these two groupings?*

• *How can knowing what gives your life meaning help you set goals with your life?*

145 | 40 Goals before Age 40

Focus: Youth identify 40 things they hope to accomplish before they turn 40.

Developmental Assets Tie-in:

21—Achievement Motivation
32—Planning and Decision Making
37—Personal Power
39—Sense of Purpose
40—Positive View of Personal Future

You will need:

• a piece of paper for each young person

• a pen or pencil for each young person

Activity: Have young people create two columns on their piece of paper, numbering the first from 1 to 20 and the second from 21 to 40.

Explain that everyone has hopes and dreams but people tend to put off what they really want to do until they're older. If possible, tell the group some of your hopes and dreams. Make sure you tell them some that you've accomplished and some that you still want to do.

Depending on your group, have young people work either in pairs or in small groups. Ask them to identify 40 things they would really like to do before they turn age 40. Encourage them to think of goals they have for the near future (such as within the next year, the next three years, the next five years, and then out from there).

Discussion Questions:

• *How difficult was it to come up with 40 goals?*

• *Which two goals can you focus on first? (Encourage young people to star those two items.)*

• *Where can you keep your list to remind you of your goals? (Explain that it's okay if lists change because people often discover new things they want to do.)*

• *Why is it important to set goals and dreams?*

• *What one thing can you do to make one dream come true soon?*

146 | A Thousand Points for Life

Developmental Assets Tie-in:

37—Personal Power
38—Self-Esteem
39—Sense of Purpose
40—Positive View of Personal Future

Imagine what it would be like if you could order the life you want on an Internet shopping site. Now imagine you have just received a gift card worth 1,000 points, and you have to spend it all to choose the things you want in life, but you can't overspend. Mark which things you would click into your "life cart."

1,000 Points for Life

	Your Cost	Add to Life Cart	Total
10 really good friends	100 points	☐	_____
A big house with all the latest electronics	100 points	☐	_____
A loving spouse	100 points	☐	_____
A healthy son or daughter	100 points	☐	_____
Belonging to a meaningful faith community	100 points	☐	_____
A college degree	100 points	☐	_____
An exciting career	100 points	☐	_____
A job with good pay and benefits	100 points	☐	_____
A pet cat or dog	100 points	☐	_____
A brand-new car of my choice	100 points	☐	_____
Good personal health	100 points	☐	_____
A vacation each year to the place of my choice	100 points	☐	_____
A good relationship with my parent(s) or guardian(s)	100 points	☐	_____
A chance to make a positive difference in the life of another person	100 points	☐	_____
A great wardrobe	100 points	☐	_____
Money to give to my favorite charities and causes	100 points	☐	_____
All the money I'll need to meet my and my family's needs	100 points	☐	_____
Other item of your choice: _____	100 points	☐	_____
GRAND TOTAL		**=**	**1,000**

147 | Tearing Down Walls

Focus: Youth name barriers to their goals and then tear down those walls.

Developmental Assets Tie-in:

28—Integrity
30—Responsibility
32—Planning and Decision Making
35—Resistance Skills
37—Personal Power
40—Positive View of Personal Future

You will need:

• a three- to six-foot piece of butcher paper

• masking or painter's tape

• washable markers

Activity: Hang up a piece of butcher paper on the wall. Explain that this butcher paper represents a wall. It's the stuff that gets in the way of making young people's dreams come true.

Give each young person a washable marker. Ask young people to write different barriers that get in the way of their hopes, dreams, and goals. Examples could include: not enough time, not enough money, discouraging people, too tired, too busy, not the right connections, scared, or failing too many times.

Discussion Questions:

• *Which barriers are the easiest to get past? Why?*

• *Which barriers are the hardest? Why?*

• *Why does it matter if we know what the barriers are to our hopes, dreams, and goals?*

• *What one thing can you do to work around a barrier?*

Bonus Idea: As a group, tear down the wall to symbolize how young people can tear down the walls to their dreams.

148 | Your Proudest Moment

Focus: Youth name their early successes.

Developmental Assets Tie-in:

21—Achievement Motivation
32—Planning and Decision Making
37—Personal Power
39—Sense of Purpose
40—Positive View of Personal Future

Activity: Have young people get into small groups and tell about a time they are most proud of when they were successful. Maybe it was the time they caught a big fish when they were 7 years old, or when they won a trophy, or when their team won a game that they were sure they were going to lose.

Sit in small groups and have groups discuss these questions, one at a time:

• What plans did you make before this success happened?

• What are other times when you worked hard for something?

• Has there ever been a time when you've worked hard for something and didn't get what you wanted? What happened then?

• What's more important: hard work, luck, the right time, or a mixture of all of these?

Discussion Questions:

• *What did you discover about yourself through this activity?*

• *Why does it help to remember your past successes?*

• *How much power do you think you have to make your goals come true?*

• *What one goal are you striving toward now?*

• *What one step can you take toward reaching your goal?*

Developmental Assets Tie-in:

39—Sense of Purpose
40—Positive View of Personal Future

Personal goals can be short term or long term. Sometimes it's tempting to think only about the big goals, but smaller goals, such as what you will accomplish this week or this month, are also important. Consider your life in the next four weeks. Circle three of the goals listed below that you would like to work toward in the upcoming month. What steps can you take to make sure you accomplish these goals?

11
Becoming Involved in the Community

A key developmental need for young people is to be valued and to feel valuable. When young people become more involved in their schools, organizations, and communities, they see that they have important roles and can influence meaningful change. The activities in this chapter encourage youth to examine their schools, organizations, and communities, and to make them places where young people are valued and feel empowered.

Focus: Youth compile a list of available extracurricular activities.

Developmental Assets Tie-in:

17—Creative Activities
18—Youth Programs
19—Religious Community

You will need:

• access to a copy machine

• copy paper

Note:

This activity may take more than one session, especially if you have multiple schools represented.

Activity: If your school, community, or organization publishes a directory of extracurricular activities for youth, photocopy that listing for each young person in the group. If not, consider having your group put a directory together to distribute to other youth. (If the young people in your program are from more than one school, ask them each to try to find a directory for their own school.) Have each youth read through the list(s) of activities and identify one that they have never tried but that seems interesting.

Then have youth locate the adult or student leader of that activity group and find out more about it. For example, have each young person take notes on the length of time their chosen activity meets, how often it meets, what the requirements for involvement are, and how many youth are involved.

Once the young people complete their investigation, compile the findings and create a book of youth activities. Photocopy the book(s) for each youth. Depending on how much these young people get into the activity, consider making the book available to other youth in your area.

Discussion Questions:

• *What kinds of activities seem most interesting?*

• *How likely are you to get involved with one or more of these activities? Why or why not?*

• *Which characteristics of these activities make them beneficial? What are some drawbacks?*

• *In addition to knowing about available opportunities, what else would make it easier or more likely for you to get involved?*

My Idea: *"We have a middle and high school teen council that gathers on a quarterly basis to compile activities and then make recommendations to the Parks, Recreation, and Cultural Resources Board."*

—Liza Weidle, Cary, North Carolina

151 | Involvement in Activities

Focus: Youth explain why young people do or don't get involved in youth programs.

Developmental Assets Tie-in:

17—Creative Activities
18—Youth Programs
19—Religious Community

You will need:

• paper

• a pen or pencil for each group

Activity: Form two groups. Give each group a piece of paper and something with which to write. Have one group focus on activities in your setting (whether you're part of a school, youth organization, or faith community) and have the other group work on community activities. Explain that each group should make a list of the benefits of getting involved in youth programs and a list of why young people don't get involved.

After groups finish, have them read their lists to the entire group.

Discussion Questions:

• *Which is easier for youth to get involved in: school or community activities? Why?*

• *Are there programs in our community that are more popular than others? Why?*

• *Why is it important to get involved in youth programs?*

• *What keeps youth from getting involved?*

• *How can you overcome some of the barriers to involvement?*

• *What are some reasons youth do get involved in some programs?*

• *How could we encourage more youth to see the benefits of program involvement?*

Developmental Assets Tie-in:

17—Creative Activities
18—Youth Programs
19—Religious Community

List each extracurricular activity, sport, club, or organization that you're involved with in your school or community. Next to each activity, write the approximate number of hours per week you spend with this organization. (If the activity happens only monthly, divide that time into four to find the weekly total. Or, if you're involved in an activity four times a year, figure out the average number of weekly hours that activity entails.) Then add up the hours at the bottom. How close are you to spending three or more hours a week doing extracurricular activities? Under each activity, write ways the activity helps you (for example, make friends, learn skills, plan for a career, stay fit).

Hours per Week _____

Activity Name _____

How It Helps Me _____

_____

_____

Hours per Week _____

Activity Name _____

How It Helps Me _____

_____

_____

Hours per Week _____

Activity Name _____

How It Helps Me _____

_____

_____

Hours per Week _____

Activity Name _____

How It Helps Me _____

_____

_____

Hours per Week _____

Activity Name _____

How It Helps Me _____

_____

_____

Total Hours per Week _____

153 | Messages

Focus: Youth analyze messages about self-esteem found in magazine advertisements.

Developmental Assets Tie-in:

38—Self-Esteem

You will need:

• an assortment of magazines aimed at teenagers

Activity: Bring in magazines that appeal to teenagers. Make sure you have some that generally are targeted to males, some that generally are targeted to females, and some that are targeted to both males and females—for example, *Teen, Seventeen, CosmoGirl!, PC Gamer, Sports Illustrated Kids,* and *Teen People.* Have youth form teams of three and discuss what the magazine ads say about self-esteem.

Discussion Questions:

• *Overall, do the ads in these magazines imply that most young people have high or low self-esteem? Why do you think that is?*

• *What are the messages about self-esteem for males? Females? Is there a difference? Why do you think that is?*

• *Why does advertising work?*

• *Is it easy or hard to believe an ad? Why?*

• *Do you feel better or worse about yourself now that you've looked at the ads? Why?*

• *What can you do to develop or nurture a strong sense of self-esteem for yourself and your friends?*

154 | Thinking about Teachers

Focus: Youth talk about the ways in which teachers motivate them.

Developmental Assets Tie-in:

5—Caring School Climate
21—Achievement Motivation

Activity: Have youth form teams of three according to the first letter of their first name (for example, Anita, Arthur, and Andrea). Have the teams talk about the teachers they've had who have motivated them the most and what those teachers did to make them feel motivated.

After everyone has had the chance to talk, ask each team to report on ways teachers have motivated them. Then have youth form new teams of three according to the first letter of their last name (for example, Anderson, Aimes, and Appleby). Have youth talk about how they motivate themselves to do well in school and additional techniques they could use to stay motivated. Share some of those ideas in the large group.

Discussion Questions:

• *What did you discover about teachers who are motivating?*

• *Who motivates you more: your teachers or yourself? Why?*

• *Why is it important to be motivated?*

• *How do you get motivated to do something important that you don't want to do?*

• *How can you motivate others?*

Create two bumper stickers with messages about doing well in school. See the examples for some ideas.

Developmental Assets Tie-in:

21—Achievement Motivation
22—School Engagement

Don't Be a Fool
Study Hard in School

LEARN tO LIVE
LIVE tO LEARN

156 | Idea Storm

Focus: Youth generate ideas for improving school climate.

Developmental Assets Tie-in:

5—Caring School Climate
24—Bonding to School

You will need:

• pencils or pens

• noisemaker

• writing paper

Activity: As a group, discuss the meaning of *school climate* and identify the components that work together in a school to make it feel like a caring and healthy place to be (for example, supportive relationships between school adults and young people, good relationships among students, safe building and grounds, clear boundaries).

Next, pass out paper and pencils or pens and ask each young person to briefly describe one problem or situation at her or his school that is working against creating a caring school climate. Collect the papers.

Form teams of three and give each team three of the papers. If you have multiple schools represented, consider creating teams according to schools. Ask teams to discuss each of the papers for three minutes, recording on the paper as many ways as they can that the writer could work to improve the situation described. Sound the noisemaker every three minutes as a signal for groups to change papers. Continue until every team has responded to all the sheets.

Discussion Questions:

• *What challenges do schools face in creating a caring climate?*

• *What strengths do schools have that could help them improve their climate?*

• *What is the role of each of the following groups in strengthening a caring school climate: students, parents or guardians, teachers, administrators, other school staff, neighbors, community leaders?*

Bonus Idea: Ask each young person to describe one strength of her or his school. Teams of three can then think of actions schools could take that build on their strengths and would improve school climate.

157 | Stick to Your School

Focus: Youth name positive aspects of their school.

Developmental Assets Tie-in:

5—Caring School Climate
22—School Engagement
24—Bonding to School

You will need:

• bowl of pretzel sticks

• napkins

Activity: Gather in a circle. Pass the napkins and the bowl of pretzels around the circle. Invite each youth to take some pretzels, but ask them to not eat them yet.

Explain that when it's their turn, youth must say one good or positive thing about their school for each pretzel stick they have taken. After youth have made their remarks, they can eat the pretzels.

Discussion Questions:

• *When you hear other youth talking about your school, are most comments negative or positive? Why do you think this is the case?*

• *Do conversations among youth about school (classes, teachers, administrators, coaches, the building, and so on) shape their attitudes about school? Why or why not?*

• *What can you do when you are part of a conversation that you think is too negative?*

• *What needs to happen in order to create a positive school climate?*

• *If there are real problems at your school, what action can you take to improve things?*

Bonus Idea: Instead of focusing on your school, focus on your community.

How Are We Seen?

Developmental Assets Tie-in:

7—Community Values Youth
8—Youth as Resources

How do adults in your community respond when they meet you or other young people on the street or in a store? How do you respond to them? Try this activity to learn more about communication between youth and adults.

First, choose a greeting that you think most adults would perceive as a friendly gesture. You might look them in the eye and say "Hi" or smile and wave or nod. If you are part of a youth group, you may choose to have everyone in your group use the same greeting and then compare results.

As you try out your greeting with adults you feel comfortable approaching, observe their responses to you, including their body language as well as anything that they say. Record your observations in the chart below.

GREETING WE WILL USE: _____

Observation Record:

	Time	Place	Response from adult	Youth alone or with other youth?	Other observations
Adult 1					
Adult 2					
Adult 3					
Adult 4					
Adult 5					

SUMMARY OF MY OBSERVATIONS:

Why I think adults responded a certain way:_____

_____

_____

What do the results tell me about adults? _____

_____

_____

159 | Meet a Local Need

Focus: Youth plan and carry out an activity to collect donations for a local agency that serves children, animals, or the environment.

Developmental Assets Tie-in:

9—Service to Others
26—Caring

You will need:

• materials will be determined by project that youth choose

Note:

This activity will take more than one session.

Activity: Have youth brainstorm ideas for a service project they could do. Encourage youth to think of organizations in your community that they might want to help.

Once youth have chosen an idea and an agency to work with, determine what they know about this agency. Gather information about this group through the Internet or by visiting the organization. Report what you have learned about the needs of this group.

Brainstorm all the possible ways young people could work together to supply what this group needs. Come to a consensus on one idea and coach youth in preparing an action plan: who, what, where, when, how.

After youth have gathered the needed funds and/or items, arrange a time to visit the agency and do the project as a group.

Discussion Questions:

• Were there any surprises in this project? If so, what were they?

• How did this activity help you live out some of the Positive Values assets (assets 26–31)?

• What new experiences did you have as you completed this project?

• Why is it important to serve others in our community?

• What new insights did you gain about our community?

160 | Designer Book Covers

Focus: Youth create book covers that promote their schools.

Developmental Assets Tie-in:

5—Caring School Climate
24—Bonding to School

You will need:

• markers

• newsprint (or brown grocery bags cut to the size of book covers)

• tape

Activity: On newsprint, record the spirit slogans that teenagers say their school(s) use in cheers, banners, and stickers. Challenge youth to create some new ones that highlight their favorite positive aspects of school, or encourage youth to create a motivational message that they think is more fitting for themselves and their circle of friends. To help youth develop their ideas, ask questions such as, "What's important to you and other students?" "What are the things you'd like to change about your school?" "What are the types of messages you'd like to hear (or others need to hear) when you are at school?"

Have youth work in pairs to design book covers to use on their textbooks. Provide plenty of markers.

Discussion Questions:

• Why do schools have slogans?

• How do slogans affect students, teachers, and others (administrators, counselors, custodians) in the school? What effect do they have on people in the community?

• Can slogans make a difference in how students feel about their school? Why or why not?

• What positive messages would you convey that aren't reflected in the slogan?

Bonus Idea: Instead of focusing on your school, focus on your community.

The Social Competencies assets are attitudes and behaviors that help you get along with the people you encounter each day. Many of these same attitudes and behaviors help you and others in your community and nation become good citizens.

Who has done the best job of showing you what a responsible member of the community does? Write their names in the first list. Think about the people you respect at home, at school, and in your neighborhood. What types of things have you learned from them? What qualities do you share? Write these in the second list.

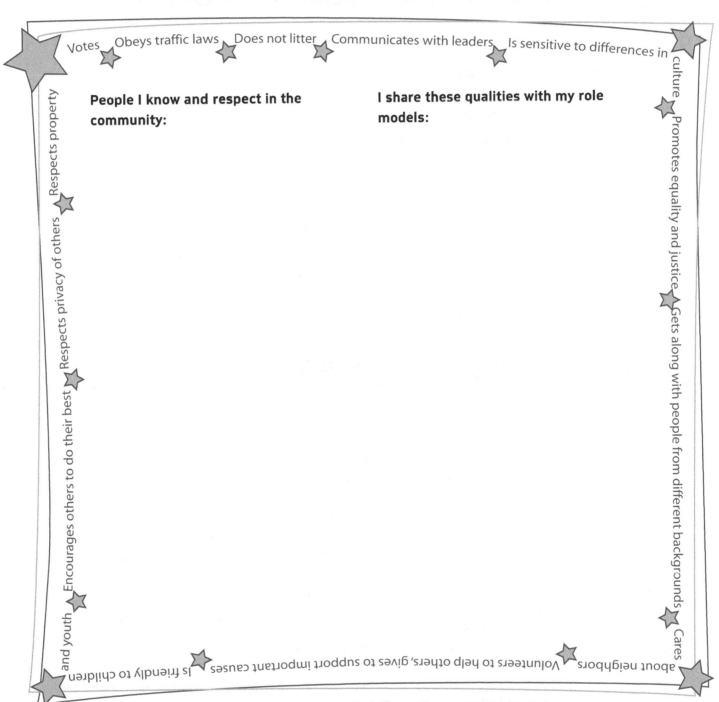

Votes   Obeys traffic laws   Does not litter   Communicates with leaders   Is sensitive to differences in culture   Promotes equality and justice   Gets along with people from different backgrounds   Cares about neighbors   Volunteers to help others, gives to support important causes   Is friendly to children and youth   Encourages others to do their best   Respects privacy of others   Respects property

People I know and respect in the community:

I share these qualities with my role models:

Developmental Assets Tie-in:
32—Planning and Decision Making, 33—Interpersonal Competence,
34—Cultural Competence, 35—Resistance Skills, 36—Peaceful Conflict Resolution

162 | Give and Take

Focus: Youth do a service project and think about how helping others builds their own assets.

Developmental Assets Tie-in:

9—Service to Others
26—Caring
27—Equality and Social Justice

You will need:

• transportation for your group

Activity: As a group, choose a service project to do together that involves direct service to people. For example, youth might choose to visit and play games with nursing home residents for a couple of hours or serve people a meal at a soup kitchen.

Discussion Questions:

After the group has completed the project, ask youth questions such as these:

• What were some of your strongest impressions about the people we helped?

• Which assets did you observe in the people we were helping?

• Which assets did they seem to be lacking? Why do you think this was so?

• Which of your own assets got a boost from doing this project? Why?

• When you give to others, what do you receive in return?

Bonus Idea: If you don't have access to transportation, consider doing a service project at your location. For example, hold a mitten drive, a toothbrush and toothpaste drive, a toy drive, a canned food drive, and so on.

163 | Making Your Area Safer

Focus: Youth discuss the safety of their neighborhood and community.

Developmental Assets Tie-in:

10—Safety
13—Neighborhood Boundaries
37—Personal Power

You will need:

• an expert from your local government who can speak about community and neighborhood safety

Activity: Before you do this activity, invite someone from your local government who represents either neighborhood watch groups or community safety plans, a community police officer, or someone who is an expert at getting residents involved in making the community a better place.

Have this person make a short presentation about how young people can make your community (or local neighborhood) safer. As a group, brainstorm a list of simple things young people can do to make their community safer and more appealing. Don't try to solve big problems; focus on small, practical steps. For example, a brainstorm list could include: helping people get to know each other, encouraging people to report suspicious activity (and knowing where to report suspicious activity), cleaning up graffiti or litter, planting flowers on community land (with permission of community officials), helping

neighbors organize a block party, and so on. Then choose one thing your group can do. Focus on what's practical and safe, and what will show results.

Discussion Questions:

• What did you learn about community or neighborhood safety?

• Why is it easy to think someone else will make our community or neighborhood safer?

• How can we measure our success with the one goal that we have chosen?

• How can we help each other reach our goal?

Bonus Idea: A week or month later, revisit this issue. Consider publicizing it through your local newspaper. See if there is anybody else who would like to get involved to further your efforts.

Think of three people you would like to help, and write one name on each of the coupons below. Then write one way you could help on each of the coupons.

For example, you might write: Dad—Help wash the dishes; or: Susan—Tutor her in math one hour this week. Be creative, and add your own designs to the coupons. After you write them, give them to the appropriate people and let them know you will be available to help them when they need it.

Developmental Assets Tie-in:

9—Service to Others
26—Caring

COUPON

FOR:_____

I can HELP BY:_____

COUPON

FOR:_____

I can HELP BY:_____

COUPON

FOR:_____

I can HELP BY:_____

Focus: Youth communicate with leaders about current events that concern them.

Developmental Assets Tie-in:

7—Community Values Youth
8—Youth as Resources

You will need:

- local and national news sections from current newspapers (at least one per youth)
- markers
- newsprint
- tape

Activity: Give each youth a marker and a newspaper to look through for stories about justice and equality issues. Ask youth to circle articles that they think report on the most important issues facing your community and nation.

Allow time for each youth to report on one article that he or she circled. Make a list on newsprint of the key issues identified.

Have youth research the names, mailing addresses, and e-mail addresses of government leaders for your community or township, state or provincial government, and national government.

Share effective communication tips with youth. Give them advice for expressing concern or offering recommendations via letter or e-mail messages with a government leader. Note these key parts of an effective message on newsprint as you present them:

- Keep your letters to one page.
- Use correct name and form of address;
- State the specific event or issue that concerns you;
- Tell why this is a concern—use "I" language to express your thoughts and feelings;
- Say what you hope the official will do (vote a certain way? speak out? study the issue?);
- Say what you will do about the issue (talk with others? correct a problem in your school or neighborhood?); and
- Thank the official for her or his time and interest.

Ask youth to work individually or in pairs to write and send a letter or e-mail to an official who is equipped to address the youth's concern. Encourage youth to bring copies of any responses they receive to a future gathering of your group.

Neighbor Search

Developmental Assets Tie-in:

3—Other Adult Relationships
4—Caring Neighborhood

Who are your neighbors? What do they contribute to a safe and enjoyable place to live? Look at the chart below. Fill in names of people who live in your area who fit each description. You can't use the name of anyone who lives in your house, and you can only use each name twice! If you have trouble with this, take some time to make connections with the people around you.

Has a great smile	Knows how to fix things	Will help if I'm locked out	Has no children living at home
Is a grandparent	Likes to chat	Bakes tasty treats	Always has time to listen
Waves at me	Comes to games or concerts at school	Has children younger than I am	Hires youth to do chores
Buys fund-raiser items	Stays calm in emergencies	Knows good jokes	Walks or bikes for exercise
Knows how to build things	Keeps an eye on what's going on	Recycles	Doesn't like noise late at night

Developmental Assets Index

Topical Index